Other books by
Seventy Fourth Street Productions:

Shakespeare's A Midsummer Night's Dream: A Prose Narrative
by Peter V. T. Kahle

Poetry for a Midsummer's Night
by Marvin Bell

Shakespeare's
THE TEMPEST

A PROSE NARRATIVE

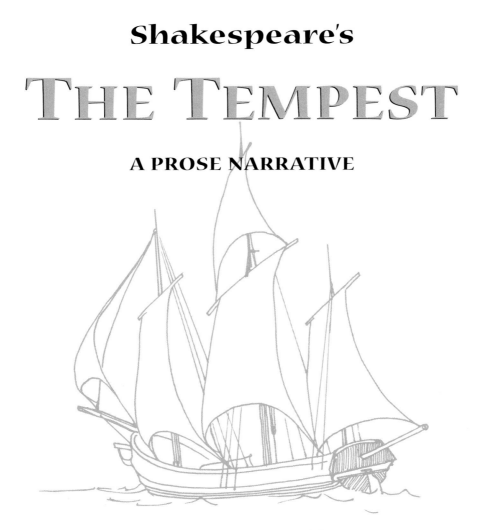

by Peter V.T. Kahle

Illustrated by Barbara Nickerson

Seventy Fourth Street Productions

Seattle, Washington

Books by Seventy Fourth Street Productions are available directly from the Publisher:

Seventy Fourth Street Productions, LLC

350 North 74th Street, Seattle, Washington 98103

206-781-1447 PHONE/FAX

www.74thstreet.com

Illustrations by Barbara Nickerson.
Watercolor on gesso, 10" x 13"

Publisher's Cataloging-in-Publication
(provided by Quality Books, Inc.)

Kahle, Peter V.T.
    Shakespeare's The Tempest : a prose narrative
/ [adapted] by Peter V.T. Kahle ; illustrated by
Barbara Nickerson. -- 1st ed.
    p. cm.
    SUMMARY: A simplified prose retelling of
Shakespeare's play about the exiled Duke of Milan
who uses his magical powers to confront his
enemies on an enchanted island.
    LCCN: 99-70763
    ISBN: 0-9655702-2-3

    1. Shakespeare, William, 1564-1616--
Adaptations--Juvenile literature.   2. Fathers and
daughters--Juvenile fiction.   3. Magicians--
Juvenile fiction.   I. Shakespeare, William,
1564-1616. Tempest.   II. Nickerson, Barbara, ill.
III. Title.

PR2878.T4K34 1999   813.54
                          QB199-82

ISBN 0-9655702-2-3

FIRST EDITION
_____

03   02   01   00   99   5   4   3   2   1

ACKNOWLEDGMENTS

For their help, I most gratefully acknowledge the following people:
Billie Escott, George and Mary Anne Fleck, Candice Fulton, Evelyn Gibb,
Joe and Hilda Kahle, Niki Kahle, Lyn Macfarlane, Jim Pravitz, Al Sampson,
Sheri Short, Shelby Siems, Frances Sonnabend, Nancy Wright,
and most of all, Lani.

INTRODUCTION

People who participate in arts activities as children are far more likely to continue to participate in the arts as adults. That conclusion, confirmed by countless demographic studies of arts audiences, motivates professional arts administrators to teach children about the arts in order to ensure future audiences. But nothing compels arts administrators and artists to engage in educational programs more than the sheer joy of unveiling to youngsters the magic, mystery and power of art.

Peter V. T. Kahle's narrative retelling of *The Tempest* is an outstanding example of how to retain the complexity of the characters and brilliance of the language in a Shakespearean play, while also making the work accessible to young minds new to Shakespeare's infinite world. It is precisely the kind of instrument that can get a youngster hooked on Shakespeare for life, and offers parents and teachers a rare shot at that sheer joy of first bringing this world to life in a young imagination.

At our Shakespeare Festival in California, we have a dual mission: to produce the works of Shakespeare and to provide classical theatre training programs for young people. While Shakespeare still is being taught in English classes, theatre and music and dance get scant attention in current curricula. Private non-profits, such as the California Shakespeare Festival, endeavor to compensate for this by offering education programs to school systems. In our case, we help teachers learn how to teach Shakespeare.

We also teach students about the performance aspects, including the disciplines of vocal and physical training, the interpersonal skills of working collaboratively, and above all the creative process of bringing a character to life on stage. After the training sessions, students attend a matinee performance of a play at our 545-seat outdoor amphitheater. Training students and teachers in the values and practices of Shakespeare, then having them attend our production, brings our dual mission into synthesis.

Every child loves a good story. And nobody tells a story better than Shakespeare. But Shakespeare's stories contain unfamiliar language and references, especially for youngsters. In our education program development, we seek to bridge the gap between great stories and young people's ability to connect to them. Kahle's narrative is an excellent step across that bridge.

If Kahle's version of *The Tempest* provides such an experience for even one child, then it is of inestimable value. I believe it will provide that experience for many children. I believe and hope this not only because an appreciation of Shakespeare creates future audiences, but also because it creates richer, deeper people.

Frank Mack
Managing Director
California Shakespeare Festival

November 7, 1998

PROLOGUE

Do you believe in magicians? Not the kind that takes a quarter out of your ear, or does card tricks, but a real magician, with a leather-bound book of spells, and a staff of power, and a cloak of blue velvet embroidered with shining silver stars and crescents.

The Tempest is a play about magic and a wild deserted island in the middle of the sea. It is the story of Prospero, Duke and ruler of Milan, stranded by his enemies upon that island with none for company save his three-year-old daughter, Miranda. Twelve years they endured, while Miranda grew wise under her father's teaching and beautiful as a rose; and Prospero studied his magic arts and gained great power. This is a tale of revenge and true love, about a wise magician, an angry monster, a grief-stricken king, a handsome prince, a beautiful maiden and two treacherous brothers. For one day it came about that his enemies sailed within Prospero's reach, and this is what happened thereafter.

When you enter a theatre, you are stepping across the border into a place where magic happens, even if the play is a true story that took place last week. A play is actors getting up in front of an audience and pretending to be someone else. And the wonderful thing about plays is that the audience pretends, too; they say, "Yes, you are Prospero, once Duke of Milan." That's when the magic happens. That's why going to the theatre is so exciting.

The actors in a play must work especially hard. They have to memorize every word that they will say on stage, and then speak their lines naturally, as if the sentences just came into their heads that minute. Four hundred years ago, a man named William Shakespeare wrote great plays about exciting characters, but the reason they are still performed today is because he used his words so well. He was a poet. He wrote his plays in verses and rhymes, and he used unusual words because of their beautiful sounds.

Sometimes Shakespeare changed the order of the words in his sentences because he liked the rhythm they made, or the way they worked. During the storm at sea which begins this story, when the Boatswain says to angry Sebastian, "Work you, then!" he means, "Then you work!" He says it that way because "work" is the word that will make Sebastian angriest. You may find it easier to understand if you read it out loud. That's what the actors do when they start to learn their parts.

Some of the words sound different from the way people talk now. During the four hundred years, some words have disappeared and we don't use them any more. Worse, some have changed their meanings. When we say *pinch* we think of just a little nip of the fingers, but long ago it could mean being arrested, or even pinched with iron tongs in a torture chamber. *Brave* also meant splendid or handsome, *art* could mean skill or learning, a *cell* might be a hermit's one-room cave or a place to put prisoners, and a *catch* could be a basket of fish, or a song. There is more about words in the Glossary on page 94.

People of Shakespeare's time felt that good and evil pressed hard upon them every hour. In those days, if any man did a bad deed, a sin, he must feel shame for it, and regret doing it, and give up any advantage he gained from his wickedness. This was called *repentance*. People believed they would be punished after they died if they had not repented all evil done in their lifetime. If they repented, they would be forgiven.

The first theatres were built in London about the time of William Shakespeare's birth. Half of his plays were first performed outdoors, in roofless theatres or the courtyards of inns, under the sunlit sky. *The Tempest* was one of his last plays, and it was played indoors, in the upper hall at the old abbey at Blackfriars. Indoors, the actors could control the light and darkness, and make scenery safe from wind or rain. Shakespeare could write a tempest, with lightning and great waves, magic and a disappearing banquet. The players could act it on the stage, protected from real weather.

The actors who first performed *The Tempest* memorized every word, every gesture, every step they would take upon the stage, just as actors do today. They wore wonderful costumes that took the breath away to see, though truth to tell, there was much paint and gauze and fool-your-eye. But when the actors looked out from the bright-lit stage upon the sea of faces, the audience believed, and the actors made that belief into magic, the same way that actors do today. Go to the theatre and see.

Sit down in your seat, but be ready for adventure. You and all the rest of the audience have entered an imaginary world, where spirits cloud the mind. You have stepped across the border to a lonely island, where wise Prospero waits with his daughter upon the rocky shore, and only the magician can say what is real, and what is an illusion.

CAST OF CHARACTERS IN THE PLAY

Dramatis Personae

PROSPERO	*magician and rightful Duke of Milan, in exile on the island*
MIRANDA	*daughter to Prospero*
ARIEL	*a spirit of the air, servant to Prospero*
CALIBAN	*a witch's son and monster, slave to Prospero*
FERDINAND	*a Prince, son to the King of Naples*
ALONSO	*King of Naples*
SEBASTIAN	*brother to the King*
ANTONIO	*the false Duke of Milan, brother to Prospero*
GONZALO	*an honest old counsellor to the King*
ADRIAN, FRANCISCO	*Lords; gentlemen in attendance upon the King*
TRINCULO	*the King's jester*
STEPHANO	*the King's drunken butler*

SHIPMASTER
BOATSWAIN
MARINERS

CERES
IRIS
JUNO
WATER NYMPHS   *Spirits in service to Prospero*
REAPERS
HOUNDS
SHAPELESS BEINGS
UNSEEN MUSICIANS

Scene

An uninhabited island

Great waves pounded on the deck.
The ship reeled from the blows.

ACT I

Scene 1

KING ALONSO OF NAPLES WAS STORM-CAUGHT AT SEA. No cloud or chancy gust of wind had threatened bad weather when Alonso took ship in Tunis, yet he was not halfway home when a tempest rose from nowhere to spring upon his ship like an angry beast.

Great waves pounded on the deck. The ship reeled from the blows. Screaming wind tore at the sails; lightning flashes lit the sky from side to side and left the mastheads glowing pale green with St. Elmo's fire.

Staring through the spray and smother, the shipmaster beheld a dark rocky shape.

"Boatswain!" he called.

"Here, master!"

"Fall to work or we run ourselves aground!"

"Cheerily, my hearts," shouted the boatswain to the sailors. "Take in the topsail! Tend to the Master's whistle!"

At his word the sailors leaped to their desperate task, running aloft into the teeth of the wind to wrestle the wet and kicking canvas.

Up from below came the royal party: Alonso, the King; Prince Ferdinand, his son; Sebastian, the King's brother; Antonio, Duke of Milan, and other nobles of the court. Their fine clothes flapped noisily in the wind.

"Good boatswain," called the King, "where's the Master?"

With every heartbeat, the ship drove down upon an unknown island, where reef and rock and other deadly dangers lurked. The boatswain was in charge of all the sails and rigging, and every man aloft in the storm. He had no time to waste in courtesy, even to the King. "I pray now, keep below," he answered, shortly.

Duke Antonio stepped forward with his hand upon his dagger. "Where is the Master?" he demanded.

"Do you not hear his whistle? You mar our labor. Keep to your cabins. You do assist the storm."

Then said Gonzalo, the King's trusty old counsellor, "Nay, good man, be patient."

"When the sea is," replied the boatswain, turning to call orders to his men.

"Yet remember whom thou hast on board."

"No one that I love more than myself," growled the sturdy mariner. "What care these roaring waves for the name of king? You are a counsellor. If you can command these elements to silence, then we will not hand a rope more. If you cannot — out of our way, I say!"

The royal party retreated below; only Gonzalo lingered for a moment, gazing at the boatswain at work. Gonzalo said to himself, "I take great comfort in this man. He was born to be hanged, and so he will not sink this day."

"Down with the topmast," roared the boatswain. "Lower, lower!"

Then came Sebastian, the king's brother, and with him Antonio, their faces flushed and angry.

"Yet again?" asked the boatswain, as they advanced on him. "What do you here? Have you a mind to sink?"

"You bawling dog!" cried Sebastian.

"Work you, then," retorted the boatswain.

"Hang, cur," yelled Antonio, "hang, you rude noisemaker."

The boatswain brushed past him. "Lay her ahold, ahold!"

A sailor fell from the rigging, to land with a crash at the boatswain's feet. "All lost," he moaned. "To your prayers. All is lost."

"I am out of patience!" snarled Sebastian.

Antonio whined, "We are cheated out of our lives by drunken sailors and this rascal."

The boatswain paid them no heed, but rushed on to rally the men for a last attempt. Gonzalo said, "He'll live to be hanged yet, though every drop of water try to swallow him."

"We split, we split!" shrieked a wild voice. "Mercy on us! We split!"

"Let's all sink with the king," cried Antonio. He and Sebastian ran below.

Overside the sea foamed in triumph. Gonzalo said, "Now would I trade a thousand furlongs of sea for one acre of bare ground."

The next bold flash of lightning showed the mysterious island but an arrow's flight away, and swiftly did the tempest drive the ship down toward it.

A sudden madness seized the king's party. Rushing on deck once more, they ignored the seamen battling with all their strength. Instead, they seized each one some object that would float: an empty cask, a wooden crate, a hatch cover. With this for his support, every man of them leaped overboard, and struck out swimming for the dear life towards the forbidding shore.

Only old Gonzalo was not taken by this madness; but he was loyal to his King. When Alonso jumped into the waves, Gonzalo followed after. They none of them knew what adventures awaited them upon Prospero's magic island.

Prospero stood upon a high rock,
gazing down at the wild and roaring sea.

ACT I

Scene 2

PROSPERO STOOD UPON A HIGH ROCK, gazing down at the wild and roaring sea. His tall oak staff he raised in triumph. No rain or blast of lightning came near him, no faintest breeze stirred the folds of his long cloak of magic. Grim joy marked his noble features.

Up through wind and rain climbed his daughter Miranda, a milk-white maid not yet sixteen. Her hair was whipped about her face until she scarce could see, yet she came on through the tempest. At last her hand touched, then tugged, the hem of that long blue cloak all splashed with shining suns and moons and stars.

"If by your art, my dearest father, you have put the wild waters in this roar, calm them," she pleaded. "O, I have suffered with those that I saw suffer! A brave vessel dashed all to pieces, and all the souls within her."

Prospero looked down, and his grim smile faded into real joy at sight of her he loved so well. He came down from his high place and drew her within the circle of his cloak, and straight away the wind ceased to torment her, and her every hair slid neatly into place. Down from the rock they came, into the trees that covered all the island, and so to a green clearing where the raging of the sea was but a gentle murmur in the morning sunshine.

Said Prospero to his daughter, "Child, things are not always as they seem. Lend thy hand and pluck my magic garment from me." And when she laid the heavy cloak by, he spoke to it, saying, "Lie there, my art." No longer wrapped in the stiff folds, Prospero looked more slender: less powerful, but no less noble.

He smiled at Miranda. "Have comfort," he said. "The wreck I have with magic art so safely ordered that not one soul has lost so much as a hair aboard her. Now sit with me, for thou must know further. Canst thou remember how we came here?"

"That I do not."

"Twelve year since, Miranda, twelve year since, I thy father was the Duke of Milan, and a prince of power."

Miranda looked about her at the wild deserted island, upon which she lived with none but her father — and his servant Caliban. She did not like to think of angry, ugly Caliban.

The grim smile had returned to Prospero's face. "By foul play were we heaved from our high seats, but also most blessedly were we helped to this island.

"My brother and thy uncle, called Antonio, betrayed me. I loved him next thyself of all the world!" He shook his head. "I, Prospero, the Duke, was fond of study and the knowledge of secret arts. The government I gave unto my brother. Myself I locked away within my library, and to my people I became a stranger. Meanwhiles, living like the Duke awaked in thy false uncle an evil nature, so that he wished to be the Duke himself. He made alliance with Alonso, King of Naples, who was mine enemy. Whereon a treacherous army gathered one midnight, and Antonio did open the gates of Milan to them."

Miranda gasped. "Wherefore did they not that hour destroy us?"

For a moment then she saw Prospero humbled. "Antonio dared not, so dear the love my people still bore me," he said softly. "Nor did Alonso wish to set so bloody a mark upon their business. They did proclaim to the people that I had gone a long voyage, and then bore us some leagues out to sea and set us — you but a babe of three — adrift in a tub, without tackle, sail or mast, rotten till the very rats had quit it."

"How came we ashore?"

"By God's mercy, and the goodness of man," said Prospero. "Some food we had, and some fresh water, that a noble man of Naples, Gonzalo, had provided. Being appointed master of our disposal, he did give us rich garments, linens and other necessaries, which have aided us much. So, of his gentleness, knowing I loved my books, he furnished me with volumes from mine own library that I prize above my dukedom. From them I found the power to land us on this shore, and thus were our lives preserved. And though my art doth carry but a short way over water, on this island I have power enough to ease our days."

"Might I but ever see that man," said Miranda, her eyes bright and shining. "And now, I pray you sir, for still 'tis beating in my mind, your reason for raising this sea storm?"

Prospero rose to his feet. Triumph shone from his face as an uncovered lantern. "Know thus, by accident most strange, Fortune hath mine enemies brought to this shore! And by my art I know my time has come."

Suddenly he turned to her, his hand raised. "Here cease more questions. Thou wilt to sleep."

And with a gentle sigh, Miranda closed her eyes, her head did droop, and she slept.

Prospero smiled down upon his daughter. She was his only joy, and teaching her was his chief delight. He took up his staff and donned his magic cloak, settling the heavy folds upon his shoulders. Climbing back to a point commanding all the sea, he called, "I am ready now. Approach, my Ariel. Come!"

Ariel appeared before him, Ariel spirit of the air. "All hail, great master!"

"Hast thou, spirit, performed the tempest that I bade thee?"

"To the last article," cried Ariel, long hair streaming. "At the height of storm, I turned myself to green flame and blazed about the ship. Not a soul but felt a fever of the mad. All the King's party plunged into the foaming brine and quit the vessel, then all afire with me. The King's son, Ferdinand, with hair all up-standing, was the first that leaped. After him the King, Sebastian, Antonio, Gonzalo and the rest."

"But Ariel, are they safe?"

"Look," cried Ariel, and the clouds swept back, and the winds dropped, and the seas calmed. "Not a hair perished. On their garments not a blemish, but fresher than before; and as thou bade me, in groups I have scattered them about the isle. See, there's the King's son. I have landed him by himself in an odd angle of the rock."

"And of the King's ship," said Prospero, "the mariners, say how thou hast disposed."

"Safely in harbor is the King's ship, in the deep nook, there," said Ariel, pointing to the gently rocking vessel. "There she's hid; the mariners all under hatches stowed, whom with a charm, I have left asleep."

Prospero's smile was wide and sharp. Thus began his revenge upon his enemies. The King should weep and Prospero be Duke of Milan once more, before the sun set. "Ariel, thy charge exactly is performed," said he. "But there's more work."

Ariel frowned. "More toil? Remember what thou promised."

"What is it thou canst demand?" said Prospero, frowning himself.

"My liberty."

"And I have promised it; but now, before the time be up? No more. Dost thou forget from what a torment I did free thee? Hast forgot the foul witch, Sycorax?"

"No, sir."

"And this witch, Sycorax, for many mischiefs and sorceries terrible, was by sailors left upon this shore. Thou, my slave, was then her servant. Thou wast too delicate to act her awful commands, thus she did confine you in a split pine tree, where imprisoned thou did painfully remain a dozen years. She died and left thee there shut up, alone on the island with her hag-born son."

"Yes," said Ariel. "Caliban."

"Thou knowst best what torment I did find thee in." Prospero raised his staff. "It was mine art, when I arrived and heard thee, that made gape the pine and let thee out."

"I thank thee, master, and your pardon ask."

"Do so, and after two days I will discharge thee free."

"That's my noble master," cried Ariel. "What shall I do? Say, what?"

"Go make thyself a nymph of the sea, invisible to any eye but mine, and bring me news in that same shape."

Ariel disappeared. Prospero descended to the green clearing, where Miranda slept.

"Awake, dear heart, awake. Thou hast slept well."

Miranda opened sleep-softened eyes. "The strangeness of your story put a heaviness upon mine eyes," she said, and yawned behind her hand.

"You must shake it off. Come, walk with me. We'll visit Caliban, my slave, who never yields us a kind answer."

They passed out of the clearing and through the sharp scented pines. Miranda said, "Caliban? 'Tis a villain, sir, I do not love to look on."

"But, as 'tis, we cannot do without him," replied Prospero. "He does make our fire, fetch our wood and serves in other duties that profit us."

The trees thinned before a vast rock of the island in which was torn a cave.

Before that rock they halted. "What ho, slave Caliban. Speak!" There came a sudden clatter from within, then silence. Prospero called again.

From the cave came a sulky voice, deep as dirt, rough as rock: "There's wood enough within."

"Come forth, I say. There's other business for thee. Come, thou tortoise."

Then came Ariel, to all appearance a water nymph, a slender maiden shape decked with brilliant shells, shimmering with all the colors of the sea. None could see the spirit save Prospero, who whispered a word in Ariel's ear. Prospero had many plots a-brewing.

"My lord, it shall be done," said Ariel, and vanished.

"Caliban, come forth," cried Prospero.

Out of the cave came Caliban, heavy shouldered, bow-legged, with mean slab mouth. His long hair was tangled and matted as though birds nested in it. He smelled of fish, and other things.

"A wicked dew drop on both of you," he growled. "A southwest wind blow on you and blister you all over."

Prospero shook his head. "For this tonight you shall have cramps and side-stitches and pinches thick as honeycomb."

"This anger is my right! This island's mine, it did belong to Sycorax my mother, and thou took it from me!" The ugly face twisted with sorrow. "When thou came first thou strok'st me and made much of me, wouldst give me water with berries in't, and teach me how to name the bigger light and how the less, that burn by day and night," said Caliban. "And then I loved thee, and showed thee all the isle, the fresh springs, the brine pits, the barren places and fertile."

Rage took him. "Cursed be I that did so! All evil charms of Sycorax, toads, beetles, bats come light on you. This island once was mine, and here you pen me in this hard rock, whiles you do keep from me the rest of the isle."

Out of the cave came Caliban, heavy shouldered,
bow-legged, with mean slab mouth.

"Thou lying slave, I pitied thee," replied Prospero, "took pains to teach thee how to speak, taught thee each hour some new thing or other. I did lodge thee in my home. And for this, thou raised thy hand to my dearest; thou didst seek to harm my child."

"O ho!" shouted Caliban. He showed big crooked teeth in a savage grin. "I would that I had done it, too."

"Therefore wast thou rightly penned within this rock."

"You taught me language," snarled Caliban, "and my profit is I know how to curse. The red plague take you for learning me your language."

Prospero shook his head. "Fetch us in fuel, and be quick, or I'll fill all thy bones with aches, make thee roar that beasts shall tremble at thy din."

Caliban snarled again, then muttered to himself, "I must obey. His art is of too much power." He shambled off to the woodpile.

So Prospero and Miranda passed on to their own cell: a great chamber it was, hollowed in the rock, a fine fair hall decked with the luxuries the good Gonzalo had provided for them. As they paused before the cell, Ariel came to them unseen, singing and playing most magical music. After Ariel came Ferdinand, son of Alonso the King. His clothes were fine and showed no stain or salt, yet his young face was smudged, and his eyes were red.

> *"Come unto these yellow sands*
> *And then take hands.*
> *Curtsied when you have, and kissed*
> *The wild waves whist."*

Thus sang Ariel. But though he had come safely to the yellow sands, Prince Ferdinand had no joy of his safety. Said he, "Where comes this music, from the air or the earth? Sure it waits upon some god of the island. Sitting on the shore, weeping at my father's wreck, this music crept upon me and hath drawn me hither."

Ariel sang a different tune.

> *"Full fathom five thy father lies.*
> *Of his bones are coral made.*
> *Those are pearls that were his eyes.*
> *Nothing of him that doth fade*
> *But doth suffer a sea change*
> *Into something rich and strange."*

"The song recalls my drowned father," said Ferdinand, for he thought himself the sole survivor of the wreck. Why else had no other answered to his calls? He listened to the music from no visible musician and said, "This is no mortal business, nor no mortal sound."

Miranda looked at him and something quite extraordinary leaped within her. She blinked rapidly and tried to breathe.

Her father said, "Say what thou seest?"

"What is it?" she asked. "A spirit? How it looks about! What a brave and handsome form it has. But 'tis a spirit."

"No, girl," smiled Prospero, "it eats and sleeps and hath such senses as we have. This gallant which thou sees was in the wreck. He's somewhat stained with grief for he hath lost his fellows and strays about to find 'em."

"I never saw ought else in nature so noble."

Prospero said to himself, "It goes on, I see, as my soul prompts it." He watched with pleasure, for he meant that Ferdinand and Miranda should fall in love — but not too soon. First he must revenge himself on King Alonso, and receive apology. After, their marriage would serve to bind two houses at the heart.

To the invisible Ariel he said, "Fine, spirit, fine, I'll free thee within two days for this."

Then Ferdinand did spy Miranda, framed in the soft green of a willow. So beautiful was she, in his eyes, that he was sure she was a goddess, and so he prayed to her, saying, "May I know if you remain upon this island? Instruct me then in any words or actions you require of me. O, you wonder!" Then seeing the flush grow upon her face, he said uncertainly, "Tell me if you be maid or no."

Miranda's cheek felt hot as flame. "No wonder, sir, but certainly a maid."

She spoke the language of Naples. Ferdinand cried, "My language! Heavens, I am the best of them that speak this speech."

Prospero stood forth from the trees. "The best? What were thou if the King of Naples heard thee?"

Fresh tears came into the eyes of Ferdinand. "He does hear me, and that he does, I weep. Myself am King, who, with these eyes, beheld my father wrecked."

"O mercy!" said Miranda.

"O terrible sea! Wrecked, and with him all his lords, and Antonio, Duke of Milan."

Miranda's eyes brimmed with tears, yet not so much for those supposed dead, but for the handsome young man's sorrow. He took her hand.

"If I must be King," he said, "I'll make you Queen of Milan."

Prospero looked from man to maid, and to himself he said, "At first sight they have changed eyes. Delicate Ariel, I'll set thee free for this. They are both in either's powers. But this swift business I must make uneasy lest too light winning make the prize light." For he wished his daughter to marry for love as well as policy. Aloud he said, "A word with you, young sir," while Miranda wondered at the sternness of his tone. "Thou hast taken a title not your own. I say, hast come upon this island as a spy, to take it from me."

Ferdinand, astonished, said, "No, as I am a man, not so."

"There's nothing ill can dwell in such a temple," Miranda pleaded.

Prospero raised his hand to silence her. "Speak not for him, he is a traitor." To Ferdinand, "Come, I'll chain thy neck and feet together. Sea water shalt thou drink, and thy food shall be roots and husks."

"No," cried Ferdinand, drawing his sword.

Prospero tapped his staff upon the ground and Ferdinand was struck weak as any babe.

"Put up thy sword, traitor," he proclaimed. "I can here disarm thee with this stick."

Miranda clutched his sleeve. "I beg thee, father."

"Hang not upon my garments."

"Sir, have pity."

"Silence! Not one word more," Prospero said. "Hush, thou thinkst there is no more such shapes as he, having seen but him and Caliban. Foolish girl, to most men this is a Caliban, and they to him are angels."

"My affections are most humble," she returned. "I have no wish to see a goodlier man."

"Come! Obey!" ordered Prospero.

Ferdinand sighed, his eyes fixed on Miranda's sweet, sad face. "My father's loss, the weakness that I feel, the wreck of all my friends, nor this man's threats are but light to me, might I but through my prison once a day behold this maid." Though he did not know it, those were the terms of Caliban's confinement; yet Ferdinand would welcome such a life, so strong was his love for Miranda. Caliban had no such tender feelings.

Prospero whispered to Ariel, "It works. Thou hast done well, fine Ariel." To Ferdinand he said, "Hark what else thou shalt do for me."

But it was to Miranda that Ferdinand did listen. Said she, "Be of comfort, he's of better nature than he's shown. Be patient, and 'twill change." And Ferdinand believed.

"Come, fellow. Speak not for him," said Prospero to his daughter, and hid a dark smile as he led the prisoner away.

ACT II

Scene 1

KING ALONSO OF NAPLES, SHIPWRECKED on an unknown island, advanced along the beach. The royal party came close at his heels: Gonzalo, right behind Alonso; Sebastian, the King's brother, and Antonio, Duke of Milan, following the path thus broken for them; Adrian and Francisco, gentlemen-in-waiting for the king, came last. All out of place they looked against the rugged island shore, for they were dressed in jewel-bright colors, as purple, red, green, gold or silver.

The sun stood high in cloudless sky, tiny wavelets hand in hand with gentle perfumed breezes came to shore as in a dance. Salt haze softened all sharp outlines.

Tall, hollow-eyed Alonso led on at a smart pace. He cared not a penny if his fine court shoes of soft leather were scuffed or cut. His only care was for his son. "Ferdinand!" he called, and again, "Ferdinand!" while his heart turned to lead in his chest.

Gonzalo, careless of his gray beard, followed close upon his King, running at command to search suspicious seaweed bundled in body-shapes at water's edge. Sebastian and Antonio walked carefully to save their shoes, muttering and jesting in low tones. The gentlemen stayed close at hand; they felt a safety in numbers where each man may depend upon his fellows.

A cove opened out before them, a neat notch in the rocky shoreline just large enough for a vessel to find safe harbor.

King Alonso of Naples, shipwrecked on an unknown island,
advanced along the beach. The royal party came close at his heels.

"Ferdinand!" called King Alonso. "Ferdinand!" The name climbed the stony cliffs of the cove, and fell back into silence.

Unseen, Ariel hovered over them, and with a puff of breath a wandering wave did send to wipe all trace of Ferdinand from off the beach. The King's ship nodded at anchor in the cove, hidden behind the magic of Prospero's cloak.

"Ferdinand!"

Moist sand steamed gently in the sun. Alonso, despairing, wished that he had never been crowned King.

Some men wish to be king, and think a king to be the most fortunate of men; that he may do whatever he likes. And that may be true, in small, or matters of no consequence. A king may order cherry pie with horseradish for breakfast and none will say him nay. But in matters large (if he is a good king), he does not what he will, but what he must, thinking of his country and his people before himself. Even his children become pieces he must play in the great chess game that protects his kingdom.

Naples traded much by sea. Ships set sail from the Bay of Naples to the four corners of the earth. Lately, pirates had begun to threaten the sea lanes. The King of Tunis held great power on the Barbary Coast; when he asked for the hand of Alonso's daughter in marriage, he offered protection for ships at sea. For the sake of his people, Alonso agreed. Claribel was his daughter, and she had to go from him to live far across the sea. That had been harsh enough. But now to lose her brother Ferdinand, to return to Naples and an empty palace, was more than Alonso could bear.

Gonzalo tried to comfort him. "Pray you sir, the miracle — our safe landing — is much beyond our loss."

Alonso turned away. "O, peace," he said.

Dark, sullen Sebastian spoke low to Antonio: "He receives comfort like cold porridge."

Antonio maintained his court smile for the King, yet spoke from the far side of his thin mouth. "The old man will not give up so easily."

Said Sebastian, "Look, he's winding up the watch of his wit. By and by it will chime."

"Good sir," began Gonzalo to the King.

"Ding-dong," said Sebastian. The Duke of Milan snickered quietly.

Alonso waved for silence. They stood just at that line where sand gave way to grass and then to trees, which climbed away to the heart of the island. No one moved while a man might count one hundred. Sebastian pulled a face at Antonio behind the King's back. Gonzalo looked troubled, as did the gentlemen-in-waiting.

One gentleman-in-waiting spoke up. "Though this island seem deserted, yet it is tender and delicate indeed," said Adrian. "The air breathes upon us most sweetly."

"If it were perfumed by a swamp," said Antonio.

"How lush and green the grass appears," said Gonzalo.

"'Tis tawny brown," Antonio replied. "How ugly."

"And how came we here with our garments, not drenched by the sea, but new as when first we put them on for the marriage of thy fair daughter, Claribel?"

The King made no reply. Antonio dismissed the question with a wave of his hand. Sebastian spoke low, but loud enough to be overheard. Bitter were his words. "'Twas a sweet marriage, and we prosper well in our return from it."

Gonzalo stepped before his King, to cut off this cruel attack. "Sir, is not my doublet as fresh as the first day I wore it?"

Angrily, Alonso said, "You cram these words into my ears against my will. Would that I had never married off my daughter, never traveled on the sea. O, Ferdinand, what strange fish hath made his meal on thee?" Most mournfully he gazed out over the water.

The gentleman Francisco spoke then, saying, "Sir, he may live. I saw him beat the waves under him and ride upon their backs. I do not doubt he came to land alive."

But Alonso had given way to grief. "No, no, he's gone," he said, and wiped his eyes.

"You may thank yourself for this great loss," said Sebastian. "You, who married Claribel to an African, and set us forth upon this voyage. We have lost your son. And the fault's your own."

"So is the dearest of the loss," cried the King.

"My lord Sebastian," said Gonzalo, sternly, "the truth you speak doth lack some gentleness, and the choice of time to speak it in. You rub the sore when you should bring the bandage." He turned his back upon Sebastian, and to Alonso said, "It is foul weather in us all, good sir, when you are cloudy."

Then came Ariel, unseen, playing solemn music, strange and sweet and thick as honey. All men of good will who heard that sound felt straight after a heaviness of the eyelids, most unendurable. The soft breeze sang them to sleep, one by one, Adrian, Francisco, Gonzalo, and they sank down upon the warm soft sand.

The King struggled longest. "I wish mine eyes could shut up my thoughts," said he.

"We two, my lord, will guard your person while you rest, and watch your safety," said Antonio.

And so, with thanks, Alonso closed tear-reddened eyes, and he slept. He never dreamt that evil lurked nearby. In some men there is no good will.

"What a strange drowsiness is this?" asked Sebastian.

"It is the climate," replied Antonio.

"Yet I do not find myself disposed to sleep."

"Nor I. My spirits are nimble. They fell all together, as by agreement. What might, worthy Sebastian, O, what might — ? I'll say no more." Antonio stopped, and glanced with cunning at Sebastian. "Yet I see it in thy face what thou should be. My strong imagination sees a crown dropping upon your head."

"Art dreaming?" demanded the King's brother.

"Noble Sebastian, thy fortune sleeps at thy feet."

Sebastian looked down at the King, asleep upon the sand, defenseless, then raised his face in unspoken question.

"Aye," said Antonio, smiling. "Will you grant me that Ferdinand is drowned?"

"I have no hope that he is undrowned."

"Then who is next heir to the throne of Naples?"

"Claribel."

"Claribel? She that is Queen of Tunis; she that dwells ten leagues beyond world's end?" said Antonio, eyebrows raised in mock astonishment. "That distance doth call, 'Stay in Tunis, Claribel. Wake, Sebastian!' Nay, we all were sea-swallowed, though some of us were cast forth again by destiny. We are called to perform an act, and what's to come is yours and mine to discharge."

"What stuff is this?" demanded Sebastian.

"There be others who can rule Naples as well as he that sleeps there, and lords who can chatter as much and as unnecessarily as this Gonzalo. I myself could do it." Antonio gazed at the sleepers and shook his head. "If you only knew my thought, what a sleep this might be for your rise to power. Do you understand me?"

Sebastian smiled his dark, wolfish smile. "I believe I do. I remember you did displace your brother Prospero, and wear now his Duke's crown."

"True, and look how well it sits upon me."

Wary still, Sebastian asked, "But for your conscience?"

"And where lies that? I have none," proclaimed Antonio, laughing cruelly. "Here lies your brother, no better than the earth he lies upon. If he were dead, if I with this obedient steel can lay him to rest forever, while you take off that old Sir Prudence who would call us to account —." Antonio laughed again, and pointed to Adrian and Francisco. "For these and all the rest, they'll take suggestion from us as a cat laps milk."

They had not shelter, food, or fire, those two cold-blooded men, yet they would plot murder. Sebastian clasped Antonio's hand in quick agreement. "Thy case, dear friend, shall be my guide. As thou stole Milan, I'll come by Naples. Draw thy sword. One stroke slays the King, and frees thee from all taxes due forever; and I, the new King, shall love thee."

The soft sea-breezes held their breath to hear murder spoke so coldly. Sebastian's eyes glittered, he gestured for Antonio to draw his sword. Antonio put hand to hilt, but showed no more than an inch of steel. Sebastian made no move to draw his blade at all. If Sebastian held his hand, if only the King died, and only Antonio held a bloody weapon when the others all awakened — Antonio's mind raced.

"Draw together," he said, "and when I raise my hand, do you the same."

So, slowly and deliberately, each looking the other deep into the eye, the traitors drew their swords till both blades gleamed.

Yet in that long slide of steel had come a moment swift as a dolphin's leap, and Ariel, invisible, arrived upon the beach beside Gonzalo. Soft, unearthly music played for the old man's ears only.

Ariel said, "My master through his art foresees the danger that you, his friend, are in, and sends me forth — for else his project dies — to keep them living."

And then Ariel sang into Gonzalo's ear:

> *"While you here do snoring lie,*
> *Open-eyed conspiracy*
> > *His time doth take.*
>
> *If of life you keep a care*
> *Shake off slumber and beware.*
> > *Awake, awake!"*

Antonio said to Sebastian, "Let us both be sudden," and they turned toward their victims.

Gonzalo woke. "Now good angels preserve the King," he said, and stirred Alonso, who sat up yawning.

"How now, awake? Why are you drawn?" said Alonso, seeing Antonio and Sebastian with swords in their hands.

Sebastian looked from one to the other, but dared not raise his blade to a man no longer sleeping.

"What's the matter?" Gonzalo demanded of him.

Sebastian stammered, "While we — while we stood here guarding your rest, we heard a burst of bellowing like bulls, or rather like lions. Did it not wake you?"

"I heard nothing," said the King.

"It was a din to fright a monster's ear, to make an earthquake," said Antonio, coming to Sebastian's aid.

"Heard you this, Gonzalo?" asked the King.

"Upon mine honor, sir, I heard a humming, and a strange one, too, which did awaken me. I shaked you, sir, and saw their weapons drawn." Gonzalo looked from Antonio to Sebastian, both standing stiff and unnatural. "There was a noise, in truth. 'Tis best we stand upon our guard, or quit this place."

Alonso drew himself together. "Lead off this ground and let's make further search for my poor son."

"Heavens keep him from these beasts," said Gonzalo, and he had more than four-footed beasts in mind. To bolster the king's spirits, he added, "He is sure in the island." He took his place at the King's right hand, the others fell in behind. They trooped away.

Ariel lingered in the cove to watch them go. When the last had passed from sight, a wave rose higher, washed all trace of passage from the sand. Ariel said, "Prospero my lord shall know what I have done. So, King, go safely on to seek thy son."

Caliban laid himself upon his face, and hid beneath his cloak.
Woven of rags and leaves and fish skins, this stormcape
covered him from crown just to the knee.

ACT II

Scene 2

ALIBAN COLLECTED DRY DRIFTWOOD FROM THE BEACH. He snorted and showed big crooked teeth in a scowl, though, truth be told, such effort was a waste. His face could not look more sour than nature had left it. Heavy-shouldered Caliban stacked the wood with careless speed. Long strands of his hair snagged on a branch; he threw it down unknowing, and roared with sudden pain.

"All the infections that the sun sucks up from bogs, fens, swamps, on Prospero fall and make him a disease!" he growled. Warily, he looked first this way, then that. "His spirits hear me, and yet I must needs curse him. But they'll not pinch, or fright me with goblin-shows, or pitch me in the mire, unless Prospero bids them."

Caliban clasped the great bundle of driftwood in his arms and stumped off on bow-legs toward Prospero's cell. Dune grass gave way to prickly brush and sweet bay bushes before the path entered the trees. Caliban heard a faint noise. His big ears twitched. The noise came again, yes, something moving in the brush, and a jingle like a tiny bell.

"Lo, now, lo!" he said. "Here comes a spirit of his, to torment me for bringing wood in slowly. I'll fall flat. Perchance he will not notice me."

He cast his load of wood aside and laid himself upon his face, and hid beneath his cloak. Woven of rags and leaves and fish skins, this stormcape

43

covered him from crown just to the knee, with but two faults. It stood out strange against the ground around, and yet left Caliban's bony legs bare for anyone to see.

There came another rustling from the bracken and then up from the leaves raised a pied hat, red and black, with bells upon it. The King's jester, Trinculo, spied cautiously around, for he feared himself the sole survivor of the wreck, and knew not what danger might lurk upon the unknown isle. A great dark cloud sailed toward him, set to rain not drops but buckets.

"Another storm is brewing," he said. "I hear it in the song of the wind. If it should thunder as it did before, I know not where to hide my head."

The jester edged out of the bushes with such care the thorns made almost no attempt to snare his doublet and tights. He stiffened at the sight of humpy Caliban beneath his cloak. "What have we here, a man or a fish? Dead or alive? He smells like a fish," he sniffed, "a very ancient and fish-like smell."

Trinculo walked round the curiosity. "Legged like a man, and his fins like arms. Any holiday fool would give a piece of silver to see him in the market square." He held his breath and lifted a corner of Caliban's cape, down near the legs. "This is no fish, but an islander that hath lately been struck by a thunderbolt."

Still as a stone lay Caliban, his eyes closed tight. He hoped whatever spirit this might be would pass him by, if only he did not move. Thunder rolled down the darkening sky.

"Alas," said Trinculo, shivering, "the storm is come again. My best way is to creep under his stormcape. There is no other shelter hereabout. Misery acquaints a man with strange bedfellows, till the storm be past."

Circling away from Caliban's feet, which made him hold his nose, Trinculo went round to the far side of the cloak. Breathing rapid, shallow, through the mouth to keep the smell at bay, with eyes screwed shut, he eased his head beneath the garment. Inch by inch his skinny frame did slither in; though, in the end, his legs — one red, one black — from knee down were left uncovered to the storm. The ground, which to him seemed hard and stony, was in truth the big head, and knobby shoulders and back of Caliban, frozen in hiding. Trinculo bethought him that a minute in such place might seem long as a year. He shivered till the cape shook as a leaf in high wind.

Up the path from the beach came Stephano, butler to the King. His black robe showed no sign of the sea, but his fat nose glowed red, as it did when he had taken too much wine. He sang as he walked, for he believed himself the sole survivor of the wreck, and cared not what danger might lurk upon the unknown isle.

> *"The master, the swabber, the boatswain and I,*
> *The gunner and his mate,*
> *Loved Mall, Meg, and Marian, and Margery,*
> *But none of us cared for Kate."*

He broke off the song. "This is a very scurvy tune to sing at a man's funeral. Well, here is my comfort," he said. He raised a rough wooden bottle to his lips and drank.

Ignoring the threatening clouds, he might have gone on to another tune in search of happier thoughts, but just then Caliban cried out, "Do not torment me! O!"

"What's the matter? Have we devils here?" Stephano stumbled over the hairy, crooked leg of Caliban, then righted himself and swelled out his chest. "I have not escaped drowning to be afeared now."

The voice of Caliban came from beneath his cover as if from the center of the earth. "The spirit torments me. O!" The cloak shook violently.

The butler gazed drunkenly down at it. "This is some monster of the isle with four legs, who hath got, as I take it, a fever. Where the devil did he learn our language? If I can keep him tame and get to Naples with him, he will make my fortune. He's a present fit to give to any emperor that ever trod on shoe leather."

"Do not torment me, I pray thee. I'll bring my wood home faster."

"O," said Stephano, "he's in his fever fit now, and does not talk the wisest. He shall taste of my bottle. If he have never drunk wine before, it will go near to recover him." He kicked aside the red leg and the black one, fished under the cloak and came up with the head of Caliban. "Open your mouth. Here is that which will give language to a cat."

Beneath the fish-skin cloak, trembling Trinculo said, "I should know that voice. It should be — but he is drowned, and these are devils." He shivered even more.

"Four legs and two voices — a most delicate monster," said delighted Stephano. "My fortune indeed. The forward voice is to speak well of his friends. His backward voice is to utter foul speeches. Come!" He poured more liquor into Caliban's eager mouth. "Amen! Now I will pour some in thy other mouth."

"Stephano!"

Stephano stopped short. "Thy other mouth doth call me by my name. This is a devil!"

"Stephano! If thou be Stephano, speak to me. I am thy good friend Trinculo."

"If thou be Trinculo, come forth!" Stephano cried. "I'll pull thee. If any be Trinculo's legs, these are they," he said, and seized the red and black shins. He pulled with all his strength. The jester slid out from under the fish skins and rags. "Thou art very Trinculo indeed. How came thou to be here with this mooncalf?"

"I took him to be dead, killed by a thunderstroke," said Trinculo. "I hid me under his cape for fear of the storm. But art thou not drowned, Stephano? O Stephano, two of us have escaped." And so glad was he that he was not alone, he seized his friend about the waist and danced him round and round in the middle of the path.

Stephano turned pale, then green. "I pray thee do not turn me about. My stomach is not constant."

Still beneath the stormcape, Caliban listened hard. "These be not spirits," said he, licking his chops. The wine heated him all the way down his gullet. "That's a brave god and bears heavenly liquor. I will kneel to him." And he crawled out to blink in the light of day. What had become of the storm cloud none could say, gone beyond the tree tops, or melted by the sun.

The butler poked the jester in the ribs. "How didst thou escape? I floated upon a cask of wine, a fine butt of sack which the sailors heaved overboard. Swear thy tale by this bottle, which I made from the bark of a tree since I came ashore."

Caliban tugged lightly at the butler's sleeve. "I'll swear upon that bottle to be thy true subject."

The other paid him no heed, but said, "Tell how thou escaped."

"Swum ashore," said Trinculo. "I can swim like a duck, I'll be sworn."

"Here. Swear on this," replied Stephano, thrusting the bottle into his hands; Trinculo took it and drank deep. "Though thou canst swim like a duck, thou art made like a goose." He slapped the jester on the back.

"O Stephano, hast any more of this?" asked Trinculo. By its heft, the bottle felt half-empty.

"The whole cask, man, is hid by the seaside," returned the other.

Caliban crouched before them on the sandy hard-packed dirt. "How now, mooncalf?" said Stephano. "How is thy fever?"

Caliban licked his chops again, in search of any hidden taste of wine. "Hast thou not dropped from heaven?" he asked.

Stephano, in his grandest voice, proclaimed, "Out of the moon, I do assure thee." Puffing his chest once more, he said, "I was the man in the moon."

The monster stared, mouth agape. "O, I have seen thee in her. My mistress showed me, and I do bow down to thee."

"Come, swear to that," said Stephano, and poured wine into the upraised mouth till Caliban must swallow or drown.

"I will kiss thy foot," said Caliban. "I pray thee, be my god. I'll swear myself thy subject."

"Come on, then," proclaimed the butler, advancing his foot as he had seen his royal master do. "Down, and swear."

Crawling Caliban kissed the dusty shoe. "I'll show thee the best springs. I'll pluck thee berries. I'll fish for thee and get thee wood enough." He stopped, then shook his fist in the direction of Prospero's cell. "A plague upon the tyrant that I serve. I'll bear him no more sticks, but follow thee, thou wondrous man."

Trinculo snickered. He was now fully recovered from his fear, by reason of numbing his wit with wine. "A most ridiculous monster," he jested, "to make a wonder of a poor drunkard. I could find it in my heart to beat him — but the poor monster is in drink." The monster also looked very strong and bony, and likely to hit back.

"I pray thee, let me bring thee where crabs grow, and I with my long nails will dig thee pignuts," said Caliban. "Wilt thou go with me?"

Replied Stephano, "Lead the way, without more talk." As Caliban shook out his stormcape and wrapped himself in its smelly folds, the butler drew the jester aside to the shadow of the trees. "Trinculo," he said, "the King and all our company else being drowned, we will be rulers here." They stared at each other with red-rimmed eyes, and each laughed long and loud at what he saw. "Here," said Stephano, "you shall bear my bottle. We'll fill him up again, by and by."

The wine sang in Caliban's ears, and he sang with it:

"Farewell master, farewell, farewell.
No more nets I'll make for fish,
Nor scrape trenchering, nor wash dish
'Ban, 'Ban, Ca-caliban
Has a new master, get a new man."

And he leaped and jigged round Stephano, who said grandly, "O brave monster, lead the way."

ACT III

Scene 1

WITHIN A HOLLOW IN THE PINES, not far from Prospero's cell, there lay a great snarl of driftwood logs, tangled and snagged as Caliban's hair, jumbled and tumbled just as he'd tossed them. Sun beat down in the hollow; no faintest breeze blew there.

Prince Ferdinand strained with all his might to drag another sea-bleached log free from the pile. The task set by Prospero was to stack them all neatly as carrots in a dish. Before suppertime.

The demand was beyond the strength of the strongest man on earth. The prince, though he could ride and run, and handle spear and sword, and play upon the harp, nonetheless had never worked with his hands a day in his life. Prospero did command it as a punishment for the part Ferdinand's father played in Prospero's overthrow; or so he said. In truth he really wished to see if Ferdinand would toil and sweat and suffer for his love, or if his bright eye would fade as his hands blistered.

Ferdinand paused to wipe his face. Flies taunted and stung him cruelly, and yet his eye still gleamed. "This my task would be tedious," he said to himself, "but the mistress which I serve makes my labor pleasure. O, she is ten times more gentle than her father is crabbed." He eased another log free from the tangle. One thick end he set upon his shoulder, and with aching legs did strive to drag it to its ordered place. "My sweet mistress weeps when she sees me work," he panted, "and I forget my pain."

Meanwhile, within Prospero's cell, Miranda waited for her chance. Prospero had kept her busy at her studies, yet twice she had contrived to see Ferdinand, hard at work. Her heart raced each time she saw him. She wanted to shout and laugh and cry and run as fast as legs could carry her, all at the same time.

Prospero's cell was no mean cave, no dank, dark crack within the rock. It was a fair and lofty hall, fine as any chamber in Naples or Milan. Prospero laid his book upon a table of carved wood inlaid with semi-precious stones. Miranda watched him from the corner of her eye. As her father's thought passed more and more into the page before him, Miranda from her bench slipped silently away.

Her feet, which knew each island path by day or night, passed swifter than thought toward the hollow where the wood was stored. She paused behind a tall pine tree and spied upon Ferdinand at work. Without the monstrous strength of Caliban, Ferdinand had no hope to shift the largest logs; his hands were bloodied, and his fine silk robe was torn, and yet he struggled on. Another log crashed into place. With scarcely pause for breath, Ferdinand pressed on with his hopeless task.

Miranda stepped into the open. She never knew Prospero followed, never saw him watching, hidden in the trees.

"I would the lightning had burnt up those logs," she said. Ferdinand spun round, his face ablaze with joy to see her. "O, set it down and rest you," said Miranda. "When this burns, 'twill weep for having wearied you. My father is hard at study. Pray now, rest yourself. He's safe for these three hours."

Ferdinand toiled on. "O dear mistress, the sun will set before I may finish what I am bid to do."

"If you'll sit down, I'll bear your logs awhile," she offered. "Pray give me that. I'll carry it to the pile." She seized the end of the great log he bore and staggered with it to the stack.

She paused behind a tall pine tree and
spied upon Ferdinand at work.

She would have grasped another trunk, but Ferdinand said, "No, precious creature, I had rather break my back than you should labor while I sit lazy by."

Prospero, hiding, looking on, delighted in this seeing. The boy worked away, undaunted by the size of his task if he might but catch a glimpse of his true love. The girl cared not a raisin for his torn clothes, but sought to share his drudgery.

"You look weary," said Miranda.

"No, noble mistress. 'Tis as fresh morning with me when you are by, though it be late at night." He clasped his work-torn hands. "What is your name? I would set it in my prayers."

Said she, "Miranda." She pressed her hand against her mouth. "O my father, I have broke your command when I said so!"

"Admired Miranda!" cried Ferdinand, making a sort of joke with her name by rearranging the letters. "Indeed," he said, "the top of admiration, worth what's dearest in the world."

All flushed felt Miranda, she scarce could meet his eye.

The log he cradled in his arms as gently as a babe, yet felt not the rough splinters. "I have liked several women, but always each had some defect in her," Ferdinand declared. "But you, O you, so perfect, are created of the best. So beautiful are you, lady."

Miranda wanted to be beautiful for him, she wanted to believe he spoke the truth, but did not know. "No woman's face do I remember, save from my own looking glass. Nor have I seen more that I call men than you, good friend, and my dear father. Yet I would not wish any companion in the world but you." She turned away. "But I prattle too wildly, and my father's orders I do forget."

The log slipped from his blistered hands and thudded on the ground. Ferdinand looked down upon his ruined clothes and shook his head. "I am in my own country a prince, Miranda; a king if my father be drowned — I would it were not so! — and would no more endure this wooden slavery than to suffer filthy flies blow into my mouth. Yet the very instant I saw you my heart did fly to be your slave, and for your sake am I this patient log-man."

"Do you love me?" she gasped.

"I do love, prize, honor you," he said, most humbly.

Tears filled her eyes. "I am a fool to weep at what I am glad of."

Back within the shadow of the trees, Prospero smiled. "A fair encounter," said he. "Heaven rain grace on that which grows between them."

Ferdinand strove to comfort her. "Why do you weep?" he asked.

"At mine unworthiness, that dare not offer what I desire to give, nor take what I shall die to want." Miranda summoned all her courage. "I am your wife, if you will marry me," she said most shyly, "but I'll be your servant whether you will or no."

This was not the way of fine court manners in Naples, where who loved whom was played at, like a game of tag; yet Ferdinand found it better. He bowed a true princely bow. "My mistress dearest."

"My husband then?" she asked.

"Ay, with a heart full willing," he replied. "Here is my hand."

"And mine, with my heart in it." And she placed her small hand in his work-scarred palm. They gazed into each other's eyes with so much care the sun did slow his passage 'cross the sky to watch. Her friends, the seabirds, wheeled above them.

With a start, Miranda recalled her father at his studies. She must return before he looked for her again. "And now farewell," she said, "till half an hour hence."

"A thousand thousand farewells," replied Ferdinand, and watched her out of sight. Then with a sigh, turned back to all his labors. Yet such comfort, strength and joy had flowed from her hand into his, he felt in truth as fresh as early morning.

Prospero, noting every speck of this, his pleasantest of plots, said, "I cannot be so glad of this as they, who are surprised by love; but nothing will rejoice me more." He whisked himself back to his cell between one eye-blink and another, that Miranda should not know he had observed her. "I'll to my book," said he, "for yet, ere suppertime must I perform much business."

Each must plunge his head full in and
drink until he had to stop for breath.

Scene 2

HE SUN SLID DOWN INTO THE AFTERNOON. The drunken clowns — Stephano the butler, Trinculo the jester, and Caliban the monster — had walked a very long way for so small an island. First they had to refill their bottle, so back to the beach to find the cask of wine which Stephano had hidden in the brush. When they found the great cask, or 'butt,' as they called it, each must plunge his head full in and drink until he had to stop for breath, before they filled the bottle. Then off again, along paths by turns sandy, rocky or hard-packed earth, now this way, now that, fast, energetic and aimless as an ant, as Caliban's muddled wits bethought of this place or that place which would be best to show his god Stephano first of all.

No other souls did they see, in all that wandering. Ariel cared for that. The spirit had led the King's party to the far side of the island; and with a breath wove branches tight to bar passage toward the clearing where Ferdinand hauled the logs. Caliban himself led his new master by ways designed to shield them from Prospero's eye.

They rested in the shade of the trees. Trinculo shook the bottle, shook his head until the bells of his red and black jester's cap jingled; he looked a question at Stephano.

Stephano waved his hand. "When the butt is empty we will drink water; not a drop before. Drink up. Servant monster, drink to me."

"Servant monster? The folly of this island!" said Trinculo. "They say there's but five upon this isle, we are three of them. If the other two be brained like us," he sniffed, "the state totters."

"Drink, servant monster, when I bid thee," said Stephano, seizing the bottle from the jester and holding it over Caliban's head. Caliban's eyes were red, and watered, and didn't focus on the bottle very well. He kept getting his nose in the way when Stephano poured the strong wine, called sack. The butler laughed. "Thy eyes are almost set in thy head."

By set, he meant staring and glassy, but Trinculo made a pun to make fun of him. "Where else should they be set?" he jeered. "He were a brave monster indeed if they were set in his tail."

Stephano replied, "My man monster hath drowned his tongue in sack. For my part, the sea cannot drown me. I swam five and thirty leagues before I came to shore." That was a great fib, for no man could swim that far; it is as much as a fast ship could sail in a day. Stephano waved his hand at Caliban. "Thou shalt be my lieutenant; we'll not run, Monsieur Monster."

"Nor walk neither," mocked Trinculo. "But you'll lie like dogs, and say nothing neither."

"Mooncalf, speak once in thy life," said the butler to Caliban.

"How does thy Honor? Let me lick thy shoe," cried Caliban. He flicked a pine cone disdainfully at Trinculo. "I'll not serve him," he said, "he is not valiant."

"Thou liest, most ignorant monster. I am ready to fight a constable," boasted Trinculo. "Why thou rotten fish, thou! Was there ever man a coward that hath drunk so much sack as I have today? Wilt thou tell a monstrous lie, being but half a fish and half a monster?"

Caliban appealed to Stephano. "Lo, how he mocks me! Wilt thou let him, my lord?"

"'Lord,' quoth he?" said Trinculo, rolling his eyes. "That a monster should be such a simpleton!"

"Lo, lo, again! Bite him to the death, I pray thee."

Fat Stephano's nose glowed cherry red. Each time the monster called the butler 'lord' or 'Greatness' or 'your Honor,' Stephano's gestures grew one touch grander, his voice one note more lofty. "Trinculo, keep a good tongue in your head. If you prove mutineer — the next tree," he said, and clasped his hand around his throat like a hanged man. "The poor monster's my subject, and he shall not suffer indignity."

"I thank my noble lord. Wilt thou be pleased to harken once again to the plan I made to thee?"

"That will I," said Stephano. "Kneel and repeat it. I will stand, and so shall Trinculo."

Caliban knelt down in the middle of the path, his smelly fish skin cloak trailing on the ground. "As I told thee before," he began, "I am subject to a tyrant, a sorcerer, that by his cunning hath cheated me of the island."

Ariel, spirit of the air, had been keeping watch upon these clowns. Now the spirit cried out, in the very voice of Trinculo, "Thou liest!"

Caliban showed his big crooked teeth in a snarl. "Thou liest, thou jesting monkey, thou. I would my valiant master would destroy thee. I do not lie."

Sternly the butler said, "Trinculo, if you trouble him any more in his tale, I will uproot some of your teeth."

"Why, I said nothing," replied the jester in surprise.

"Mum then, and no more," ordered Stephano. "Proceed."

Caliban snorted and glared at Trinculo. "I say by sorcery Prospero got this isle; from me he got it. If thy Greatness will revenge it on him, for I know thou dar'st, but this thing — " he tapped his chest " — dare not."

"That's most certain," muttered Trinculo.

"Thou shalt be lord of it, and I'll serve thee."

Stephano turned the plan over in his mind, which moved slowly, being awash in wine. "How shall this be come to pass? Canst thou bring me to the party?"

"Yes, yes my lord, I'll yield him thee asleep, where thou mayst knock him on the head."

Ariel laughed silently, then using Trinculo's voice once more, cried out, "Thou liest. Thou canst not."

Caliban ground his teeth with rage. "What a pied ninny is this! Thou scurvy patch! — I do beg thy Greatness, give him blows and take his bottle from him. He shall drink naught but brine, for I'll not show him where the fresh streams are."

Stephano raised his fat fist in warning. "Trinculo, interrupt the monster one word further, and I shall beat thee like a drum."

"Why, what did I?" protested Trinculo. "I did nothing. I'll go further off."

"Didst thou not say he lied?"

Ariel, delighted, used Trinculo's voice once more. "Thou liest."

Stephano's whole face blazed to match his nose. "Do I so?" he roared. "Take thou that!" He slapped Trinculo's face, and knocked his pied hat off. He grabbed the jester's long nose and twisted it, and kicked his backside. "As you like this, give me the lie another time."

"I did not give the lie!" whined Trinculo. "Out of your wits and hearing too? A pox on your bottle! This can drinking do. A plague on your monster and the devil take your fingers!"

Caliban laughed to see him beaten so.

"Now forward with your tale," said Stephano.

"Beat him enough," answered Caliban. "After a little time, I'll beat him, too."

"Come, proceed," said the butler, swirling his fine black gown around him.

"Why, as I told thee, 'tis a custom with Prospero in the afternoon to sleep. There thou mayst brain him. Remember first to seize his books, for without them he's but a fool, as I am, nor hath not a spirit to command. They all do hate him as much as I. Burn naught but his books. He has brave furniture and silver candlesticks and other goods." The monster stopped. "And that most deeply to consider is the beauty of his daughter," he said. "He himself calls her beyond compare."

"Is she so brave a lass?"

"Aye, lord," answered Caliban.

Stephano considered once more. His face lighted with his decision. "Monster, I will kill this man. His daughter and I will be king and queen, and Trinculo and thyself shall be viceroys. Dost thou like the plot, Trinculo?"

"Excellent," said Trinculo, but without much heart.

Stephano moved to make up with him. "Give me thy hand. I am sorry I beat thee. But while thou live, keep a good tongue in your head."

Caliban danced round them, impatient. "Within this half hour he will be asleep. Wilt thou destroy him then?"

"Aye, on my honor," proclaimed the butler, already seeing a crown upon his own head.

Observing all, Ariel, invisible, considered. The spirit did not hate Prospero. Ariel said softly, "This I will tell my master."

Caliban clapped great hard hands in glee. "Thou mak'st me merry, I am full of pleasure. Wilt thou sing the catch thou taught me?"

So pleased at thought of crown and queen awaiting him for just a little bloodshed, Stephano answered, "At thy request, monster, I will do it. Come Trinculo, let us sing."

They tried, but it sounded worse than dogs howling. "That's not the tune," the butler cried, breaking it off. For the wine had got to their throats, and they could not carry a melody in a basket.

Ariel smiled, and caused first a hidden pipe to play that self-same catch the clowns had failed to sing, and next a tabor to sound, small drum unseen that set a cheerful beat.

"What is this?" Stephano asked of Caliban.

Trembling Trinculo searched the woods around them and saw — no one. "This is the tune of our catch played by the picture of Nobody," he quavered.

Brash Stephano raised his voice. "If thou be'st a man, show thyself in thy likeness. If thou be'st a devil, take it as thou wilt."

"O forgive me my sins!" prayed the jester.

"He that dies pays all debts. — I defy thee!" shouted Stephano, trying to appear bold. Yet he cried, "Mercy upon us," when Caliban tugged his sleeve unexpectedly.

"Art thou afeared?" asked Caliban.

"No, monster, not I," said the butler, though his legs quaked.

"Be not afeared," said Caliban. "The isle is full of noises, sounds and sweet airs that give delight and hurt not. Sometimes a thousand twangling instruments will hum about mine ears," he said, and for a wonder his face almost looked gentle. "Sometimes voices sing, that, if I then had waked after long sleep, will make me sleep again; and then, in dreaming, the clouds methought would open and show riches ready to drop upon me, that when I waked I cried to dream again."

Stephano hardly heard him. He drank from his bottle. "This will prove a splendid kingdom to me, where I shall have my music for nothing."

Caliban tugged his sleeve. "When Prospero is destroyed."

Stephano drank once more. The island was so fair, the wine so good, he could hardly keep business to mind. "That shall be by and by. I remember the story."

The strains of Ariel's music drifted slowly away from them, leading down-hill, through the trees, away from Prospero's cell.

Trinculo, jester and musician himself, was most captured by Ariel's music. "The sound is going away," he said. "Let's follow it, and after do our work."

The afternoon was soft and warm. Stephano agreed. "Lead, monster. We'll follow. — I would that I could see this taborer. Wilt come?" he said to Trinculo.

"Yes, I'll follow, Stephano."

ACT III

Scene 3

LL THAT TIME, WHILE STEPHANO, TRINCULO and Caliban had been getting drunk, and Ferdinand and Miranda had been falling in love, the King had been searching for his missing son. Alonso's robes of royal purple were smirched and torn about the hem, his soft shoes were cut and scuffed, but the King cared not, so keen was he to find Ferdinand. Yet the sun had swept half-way from noon to suppertime, and still he had seen no sign of the missing Prince.

Alonso walked as in a daze, hardly speaking when spoken to. His whole soul focused through his eyes; he stared at every rock and shrub and tree as if to pierce it through. The royal party straggled after. Gonzalo's aged legs could no longer keep him in his place of pride at the King's right hand. He fell behind the gentlemen, Adrian and Francisco, and gasped for breath. The gentlemen were but little better off themselves.

Far behind idled the King's brother, Sebastian, and Antonio, Duke of Milan. They kept their eyes upon the King's back, and their hands upon their daggers. They had made plans to kill the King and old Gonzalo, and only Ariel had prevented them. They did but wait another opportunity to strike.

At last the King and his men came to the far side of the island, well removed from Prospero's cell. They had searched every inch of ground that Ariel had permitted them; and so thought that they had seen the isle entire.

When they stepped out of the trees, sight of the sea took from Gonzalo his last strength.

"By our Lady, I can go no further, sir," he said. "By your patience I must rest."

"Old lord," said the King, "I cannot blame thee, who am myself seized with weariness. Sit down and rest."

Gonzalo sank upon the green grass. Adrian and Francisco ran to stuff a cloak with leaves to make a cushion for Alonso. Sebastian and Antonio approached, paying no attention to anything but the ground around their feet, for they wished to keep their shoes clean.

"I will put off my hope and keep it no longer." The King could not take his eyes from the sea. A tear ran down his cheek. "He is drowned whom we do stray to find, and the sea mocks our useless search. Well, let him go."

The gentlemen knelt down before him, but behind Alonso's back, the Duke of Milan nudged Sebastian. "I am right glad that he's so out of hope," said Antonio, softly.

Tapping his dagger, Sebastian whispered, "The next advantage we will take."

"Let it be tonight," said Duke Antonio, "for now they are worn with travel, they cannot be so watchful as before."

Prospero gazed upon them, his cloak of magic draped about his shoulders, his wizard's staff gripped in his strong hand. He stood so close that he did mark their every word or gesture, yet he was wrapped within his magic arts, and so they saw him not.

Then came to them the strains of slow and solemn music, beautiful and strange. "What is this?" asked the King. "My good friends, hark."

"Marvelous sweet music!" said Gonzalo.

Out from the shade of the trees danced several strange shapes, beings part man, part animal. They were Prospero's lesser spirits, come to help with this part of his revenge.

Gonzalo moved to stand beside the King; Sebastian and Antonio took shelter behind him. The shapes, though monstrous, made no attack, but laid a table on the grass before the King's party, and on it placed such wondrous food and drink that none there had ever seen better. There were roasted peacocks, with the feathers all carefully replaced so that the bird lay in its dish even as it looked in life; boar's heads with tusks all gilded gold; great pasties shaped like castles, with pie-crust battlements and spun-sugar soldiers; and there were gleaming mounds of apples and pears and all delicious fruits. The hungry men could hardly trust their eyes, yet such aromas reached them that their mouths did water.

Shaken by sight of this oddness, the King said, "Guardian angels protect us! What are these?"

The others gaped all open-mouthed. Gonzalo shook his head. "If in Naples I should report this now, would they believe me?" He gestured toward the servers. "Though they are of monstrous shape, yet note their manners are more gentle, kind, than of our human generation."

Prospero, looking on, murmured to himself, "Honest lord, thou hast said well, for some of you there present are worse than devils."

The King said, "I cannot help but wonder at such shapes, such gesture, and such sound, expressing without tongues a kind of excellent silent language."

A grim smile lit Prospero's noble face. His plan had more to come, from which these nobles would take no delight.

Prospero's strange servers danced most gracefully, and with many bows and outstretched arms made invitation to the feast so magically prepared. Then did they disappear once more into the trees.

*The shapes, though monstrous, laid a table on the grass before
the King's party, and on it placed such wondrous food
and drink that none there had ever seen better.*

The gentleman Francisco turned to the King. "They vanish strangely," he said.

Sebastian grew brave once the spirits had gone. "No matter, since they have left their foods behind, for we have stomachs." He turned to his brother, Alonso. "Will it please you taste of what is here?"

"Not I," replied the King.

"Faith, sir, you need not fear," said old Gonzalo. "When we were boys, who would believe such tales? Yet we have found wonders to be true."

None of his party would eat unless the King did, so at last he gave consent. "I will stand to and feed. If it be my last meal, no matter, since I feel the best is past," he said, mourning for lost Ferdinand. "Brother? My lord the Duke? Stand to, and do as we." And he stepped up to the table.

A great crack and rumble of thunder split the air. Darkness as a carpet rolled across the sky. Stock-still the royal party stood in full amazement. By the weird green storm-light then they saw a huge winged shape descend upon the table. Strange woman's face it had, all twisted with rage, and wide wings, dull gray and plumed like a vulture; sharp talons that gripped the table till the very boards cried out in pain. Ariel it was, who had come before them in the shape of a Harpy, cruel avenger of the ancient world. Such creatures come upon wanderers lost and in peril, to devour or destroy the food of starving men, and scream dire prophecies about their fate. Two other terrors circled overhead, and where their shadows fell, men shivered.

Harpy Ariel clapped wings upon the table and the banquet vanished, leaving not a crumb upon the cloth.

In a voice deeper than the thunder, the Harpy cried, "You are three men of sin. Destiny hath caused the sea to belch you up upon this island, where man doth not inhabit; you being most unfit to live amongst men. Here I will drive you to madness."

Alonso, Antonio and Sebastian drew their swords.

The Harpy laughed a terrible laugh. "You fools, I and my fellows are agents of Fate. Your swords may as well wound the loud winds or stab the still-closing waters as bend one feather in my plume. If you could hurt, your swords are now too massive for your strengths, and will not be uplifted."

And on that word, not one of the three could lift his sword point from the ground, though they strove with all their strength.

"Remember!" cried the Harpy, "for that's my business to you — remember that you three from Milan did overthrow the good Prospero, exposed him unto the sea, him and his innocent child! For this foul deed, the powers — not forgetting — have enraged the seas and shores, yea, all the creatures against your peace. Thy son, Alonso, they have ripped from thee; and you shall linger in the ruin of your hopes, worse than any death can be at once, in this most desolate isle, with nothing but heart's sorrow and long life ensuing."

Then with a greater thunder clap than any yet they'd heard, the Harpies vanished. Once more the royal party heard that soft strange solemn music. Once more the spirits came from out the trees, yet now their dance was mean and mocking, their gestures insolent and cold. They bore away the table and disappeared. The sun shone brightly again in the late afternoon sky.

Sebastian and Antonio at once raised high their swords, and threatened the empty air. But Alonso, stricken, let his blade fall from his hand. His guilt was written plain upon his face.

Prospero, observing the success of this, his revenge, said to himself, "Bravely the figure of this Harpy hast thou performed, my Ariel. Thou hast followed my instruction to the word. My high charms work, and these, mine enemies, are all knit up in their distractions." He watched the two villains swing their swords, while the King's face twisted with sorrow and remorse. "They now are in my power; and in these fits I leave them, while I visit young Ferdinand, whom they suppose is drowned. He sits with his and my loved darling." And drawing his cloak about him, he left them there.

Gonzalo, who of his gentleness had no crimes upon his conscience, was unaffected by the spell, as also Adrian and Francisco. To the King, the old counsellor said, "In the name of something holy, sir, why stand you in this strange stare?"

Replied Alonso, "O, it is monstrous, monstrous! Methought the billowing waves spoke and told me of it; the winds did sing it to me and the thunder, that deep and dreadful organ pipe, pronounced the name of Prospero. O the baseness of my treachery!" His eyes had filled with tears. "Therefore my son in the ooze is bedded, and I'll seek him deeper than ever anchor sounded, and with him there lie mudded." He turned and ran down toward the beach.

Sebastian waved his sword, and dared the Harpies to return. He felt no guilt or sorrow. His one thought was to kill anyone who charged him with his crime. "One fiend at a time," he shouted. "I'll fight their legions over."

Antonio was just as bad. "I'll be thy second," he yelled. They ran after the King.

Gonzalo and the gentlemen-in-waiting stared after them. Gonzalo said, "All three of them are desperate. Their great guilt, like poison, now begins to bite their spirits." He turned to young Adrian and Francisco. "I do beg you that are of suppler joints, follow them swiftly and hinder them from what this madness may now provoke them to." He feared Alonso might cast himself into the sea, or that Sebastian and the Duke might carry out their plot.

"Follow, I pray you," replied Adrian, and the three of them set out to catch up to the King.

ACT IV

Scene 1

PROSPERO'S CELL WAS CARVED into the living rock of the island. Out from his door there spread a fan of short, springy turf, a half circle of green lawn walled about by tall dark trees. Two paths did pierce the wall, west and east. Through the western entry flowed clear shafts of sunlight. Late afternoon glowed rich butter yellow in the clearing.

Miranda waited for her father to return, who had gone to fetch Ferdinand from his labor in the logyard. She waited in the sunlight, her eyes closed, not quite praying, not quite dreaming. Ferdinand said he loved her. Prince Ferdinand of Naples, if he were to be believed, and Miranda believed every word he said. Possibly even King Ferdinand, if his father had drowned in the shipwreck. Ferdinand believed he was drowned. Miranda was puzzled about that. Prospero had told her that no one was harmed in any way by the storm, and Miranda believed him, too. All her life, Miranda had known nothing but love and wisdom from her father. But now there was Ferdinand. The sun was warm upon her face. Ferdinand said he loved her, and would be her husband — if Prospero would agree.

And he had not yet agreed. She held her eyes shut against disappointment. Her father's old grievance barred the way. The King of Naples had helped to overthrow Prospero, he had stood by while the wicked Antonio set Prospero and three-year-old Miranda adrift in an open boat on the open sea.

Slanting sunbeams lit Miranda
with a golden light.

This shipwreck on the island was her father's revenge. She knew not what had become of the King, but all day Prospero had made Prince Ferdinand toil in chains.

She heard her father's voice before they came into the clearing. When she opened her eyes she could scarce believe them, for noble Prospero, his cloak of magic folded across his arm, led Ferdinand as an honored guest. Tired, aching, excited, tattered and joyous Ferdinand.

Prospero said to him, "If I have too severely punished you, your reward shall make amends, for I have given you here a third of mine own life, or that for which I live. All thy vexations were but my trials of thy love, and thou hast stood the test." Her father smiled at Miranda, and held out his hand to her. "Here, afore heaven is my rich gift. O Ferdinand, do not smile at me that I boast of her, for thou shalt find she will outstrip all praise and make it halt behind her."

Slanting sunbeams lit Miranda with a golden light. Ferdinand looked at her kneeling, glowing, and knew that he had found his one true love and heart mate. "I do believe it," he said, "against any oracle or fortune ever cast."

"Then as my gift and thine own prize well won, take my daughter," said Prospero, and joined her hand to Ferdinand's. "Be restrained," he said, in that way in which well-meaning fathers embarrass their daughters. "Be restrained, thou art not man and wife until the full and holy ceremony's held."

Ferdinand laughed. "As I hope for quiet days and long life, with such love as 'tis now," he said, gazing into Miranda's eyes, "I will be content until the day of celebration."

"Sit then and talk with her. She is thine own."

Miranda drew Ferdinand aside to tend those sore hands which had won her father's favor. While they were distracted, Prospero stepped away.

"Ariel, my industrious servant, Ariel!" he called.

Ariel appeared, visible to his eyes only. "What would my master? Here I am."

"Thou and thy lesser fellows your last service did worthily perform," said Prospero, meaning the magic banquet and the harpy, "and I must use you for such another trick. Go bring those spirits here to this place. I will bestow upon the eyes of this young couple some vanity of mine art."

Ariel sang:

"Before you can say 'Come' and 'Go,'
Each one, tripping on his toe,
Will be here with mop and mow.
Do you love me, master? No?"

"Dearly, my delicate Ariel," laughed Prospero. "Do not approach till thou dost hear me call."

"I understand," said Ariel, and was gone.

Prospero led his daughter and Prince Ferdinand across the clearing to several soft couches set in a group, and there he seated them. "Well. — Now come, my Ariel. Bring all rather than lack a spirit. Appear, and pertly."

Soft music began to play. Miranda looked to her father to speak, but he said, "No tongue. All eyes. Be silent."

So began the masque of Prospero's devising. A formal entertainment, very much admired at the courts of Naples and Milan, a masque is a simple play of actors and actresses portraying gods and goddesses from ancient times, with poetry, music and dancing. At a wedding feast or some such glad event, these goddesses might speak blessings on the happy couple.

Out from the trees, as though onto a stage, stepped Iris, spirit of the rainbow, many-colored messenger to the gods of old Olympus. And she was clothed in all the colors of that rich scarf that drapes the drying earth. With ringing verses she called to her side Ceres, goddess of the harvest, who came wearing grape leaves for a crown, and in her hand she held a single golden stalk of wheat. Together they waited upon Juno, Queen of the Sky, and Juno came trailing clouds of glory. Ferdinand, who had seen many a masque at court, sat with mouth ajar. It was expected that the costumes would be rich and elegant, the music and dancing of the finest, but never till now had he seen true goddesses and spirits perform.

When Juno and Ceres had sung blessings on Ferdinand and Miranda, Ferdinand found his voice at last, and to Prospero said, "This is a most majestic vision. May I be bold to think these spirits?"

"Spirits, which by mine art I have called to enact my fancies."

"Let me live here ever," said Ferdinand. "So rare a wondered father and a wife makes this place paradise."

Prospero smiled at such praise, but his smile faded. "Sweet now, silence. There's more to come. Hush and be mute, or else our spell is marred."

Iris called to her side certain water nymphs, all green and silver beauties from the brooks and rivers; and she called to her certain reapers and harvesters, sunburned and dusty from the furrow and field. Unseen musicians struck up a merry country tune, and the harvest men and the water spirits danced in joy and celebration. Faster and faster they danced, while Miranda clapped her hands with delight, and Ferdinand did smile at her as though the sun rose in her eyes.

Yet in the midst of merriment, Prospero did recall the warning brought by Ariel of Caliban, and those with him, who came with murder in their hearts. If there was love in the world, there was also death. No magic art could make good fame or fortune last forever, not even for his daughter.

Prospero sighed. The minute of Caliban's plot had almost come. The time to act had arrived. He raised his hand and smote his staff upon the ground. "Well done. Avoid. No more."

And with strange, hollow and confused noises, the spirits heavily vanished.

Ferdinand and Miranda stared at Prospero, and the starkness of his face. Ferdinand said, "This is strange. Your father's in some passion that works him strongly."

Replied Miranda, "Never till this day have I seen him touched with anger."

Prospero said to Ferdinand, "You do look, my son, as if you were dismayed. Be cheerful, sir." Then he said a thing that Ferdinand did not understand. He said:

> *"Our revels now are ended. These our actors,*
> *as I foretold you, were all spirits and*
> *are melted into air, into thin air;*
> *and like the baseless fabric of this vision,*
> *the cloud-capped towers, the gorgeous palaces,*
> *the solemn temples, the great globe itself,*
> *yea, all which it inherit, shall dissolve,*
> *and like this insubstantial pageant faded,*
> *leave not a rack behind. We are such stuff*
> *as dreams are made on, and our little life*
> *is rounded with a sleep."*

Ferdinand didn't know what he meant at first, but the words stayed in his mind for a long time until he did.

Prospero strove to shake off his thoughtful mood. "Sir, I am vexed," he said. "Bear with my weakness. Be not disturbed. My old brain is troubled. If you be pleased, retire into my cell and there repose. A turn or two I'll walk to still my beating mind."

Miranda touched her father's cheek, then stepped back and took Ferdinand's hand. "We wish your peace," they said to him, and went inside the cell.

"Come with a thought. I thank thee, Ariel. Come," called Prospero.

Ariel appeared. "Thy thoughts I cleave to. What's thy pleasure?"

"We must prepare to meet with Caliban."

"Ay, my commander."

Prospero nodded. "Say again, where didst thou leave these varlets?"

Ariel laughed, a most musical sound. "I told you sir, they were red-hot with drinking, so full of valor that they smote the air for breathing in their faces. Then I beat my tabor, my little drum, at which they pricked their ears and lifted up their noses as they smelt music. So I charmed their ears that calf-like, they followed me through toothed briers, prickling gorse bushes and thorns. At last I left them in the filthy pool beyond your cell, there dancing up to the chins. The foul lake overstunk their feet!"

"This was well-done, my bird," replied Prospero. "Thy shape invisible retain thou still. Cheap flashy goods will do, bring them hither for bait to catch these thieves."

"I go, I go," called Ariel.

"Caliban! A devil, a born devil, on whom my pains taken, all, all lost, quite lost," murmured Prospero. "I will plague them all to roaring."

Then came Ariel loaded with fine sparkling clothes; Ariel had come and gone within Prospero's cell, yet Ferdinand and Miranda saw never a trace.

"Come hang them on this line," said Prospero.

They had but time to hang the garments out before the sound of drunken voices reached them from the trees. Prospero draped his magic cloak around his shoulders; he and Ariel, both concealed, stood sentry in the clearing.

In through the eastern entry staggered Stephano the butler, Trinculo the jester and Caliban the monster. Each looked as if he had been dipped into a swamp and rolled in a pigsty.

"Pray you, tread softly," whispered Caliban, his finger to his lips. "Tread softly that the blind mole may not hear a footfall. We now are near his cell."

"Monster —" said Stephano, in his normal speaking voice, though Caliban did try to shush him, "— Monster, your fairy has played the knave with us."

Trinculo whined, "Monster, I do smell all horse piss, at which my nose is in great indignation."

"So is mine," Stephano sniffed, and pushed him away. "Do you hear, monster? If I should take a displeasure against you, look you —." He clenched his fist at Caliban.

"Thou were but a lost monster," sneered the jester, pleased to see Caliban in trouble.

"Good my lord, give me thy favor still," replied Caliban. "Be patient, for the prize I'll bring thee to shall wipe out all this mischance. Therefore speak softly." He pointed toward the door into Prospero's cell. "All's hushed as midnight yet."

Remembering his bloody task, to kill Prospero so that he could marry Miranda and be King of the island, Stephano agreed. They had turned again and focused on the door when Trinculo burst out, "Ay, but to lose our bottles in the pool!"

Distracted once more, Stephano said, "There is not only disgrace and dishonor in that, monster, but an infinite loss. I will fetch off my bottle, though I be over ears for it."

Caliban danced with frustration. "Pray thee, my King, be quiet! Seest thou here, this is the mouth of the cell. No noise, and enter, do that good mischief which may make this island thine own forever, and I, Caliban, forever thy footlicker."

"Give me thy hand. I do begin to have bloody thoughts," said the butler, reaching for his dagger. It was coated with mud and slime; he tried to wipe the handle with his sleeve, which was not clean enough to help.

Then Trinculo saw the glittering clothes upon the line. Fine doublets and jerkins hung there, and velvet gowns and silks from the East. "O King Stephano, look what a wardrobe here is for thee!"

"Let it alone, thou fool," hissed Caliban. "It is but trash."

"Oho, monster, we know what belongs," said the jester, tossing aside his muddy cap. He draped a fine gown of best cloth of gold across his arm. "O, King Stephano!"

The butler took one look and laid his hand upon the sleeve. "Put off that gown, Trinculo. By this hand, I'll have that gown."

Sulky Trinculo let it drop to the turf. "Thy Grace shall have it."

"Drown this fool!" raged Caliban. "What do you mean, to dote thus on such baggage? Let it alone, and do the murder first. If he awake, from toe to crown he'll fill our skin with pinches."

"Be you quiet, monster," growled Stephano. Then with a mock bow he said, "Mistress Line, is this not my jerkin?" and pulled a fine jeweled one down.

"Do, do," said Trinculo, looking for the next richest piece, to claim it for himself. "We steal by line and level," he said, "if it please your Grace."

"I thank thee for that jest," said Stephano. "Here's a garment for it. Wit shall not go unrewarded while I am king of this country."

"Monster, come with sticky fingers and away with the rest," ordered Trinculo.

"I will have none of it," snarled Caliban. "We shall lose our time and be turned into barnacles or to apes with foreheads low and villainous."

Butler Stephano recalled that he was to be King. "Monster," he commanded, "help to bear this away where my butt of wine is, or I'll turn you out of my kingdom. Go to, carry this." He handed him the richest jerkin.

"And this," said the jester, piling on his choice of gown.

"Ay, and this," said Stephano, reaching for one more garment, when suddenly a great howl rose from the trees; wails and yelps twined with it. Out of the shade poured a whole pack of hounds, big, fierce, red-eyed dogs of chase, willing to pull down anything that moved. Trinculo threw a tangle of velvet aside and ran for dear life. Stephano raced for the path, a gown half over his head so he must peer through the arm-hole. Caliban gnashed his teeth and fled, no match for all the dogs of Prospero.

Prospero and Ariel hallooed their spirit-hounds like hunters, calling, "Silver! There it goes, Silver!" and "Fury, Fury! There Tyrant, there! Hark! Hark!"

The three clowns scrambled away with the beasts hard upon their heels.

Cried Prospero, "Go, charge my goblins that they pinch-spot these fools as any leopard."

"Hark, they roar," laughed Ariel, as a tooth nipped too close to Stephano's backside.

"Let them be hunted soundly," said Prospero, gripping his staff. He smiled grimly. "At this hour all my enemies lie at my mercy. Shortly shalt all my labors end, and thou shalt have the air at freedom. For a little longer follow, and do me service."

ACT V

Scene 1

THE SUN SETTLED TOWARD EVENING. In the clearing outside his cell, tall Prospero settled his magic cloak about his shoulders. To Ariel he said: "Now does my project gather to a head. My charms crack not, my spirits obey, and time goes upright. How's the day?"

Ariel replied, "Near the sixth hour past noon, at which time, my lord, you said our work should cease."

Prospero nodded. "I did say so, when first I raised the tempest. Say, my spirit, how fares the King and his followers?"

"All prisoners, sir. They cannot budge till your release."

Prospero's power indeed held them spellbound. Alonso the King, repenting of his guilt, believed that his betrayal of Prospero had cost him the life of his son. Alonso would have cast himself into the sea to drown but that Prospero's magic held him to the beach. Sebastian, the King's treacherous brother, and Antonio, wrongful Duke of Milan, had no repentance. Waving their swords, they raged to kill the messenger of their misdeeds, but Ariel rooted their feet that they might windmill harmlessly. The gentlemen, Adrian and Francisco, mourned over them, brimful of dismay; the good old Lord Gonzalo's tears ran down his beard like winter's rain.

Said Ariel, "Your charm so strongly works 'em that if you now beheld them, your affections would become tender."

"Dost thou think so, spirit?"

"Mine would, sir, if I were human," answered Ariel.

Prospero stood awhile in thought, for one who wields great power, as he did, cannot be mean or petty. Then he said, "Hast thou, which art but air, a feeling of their afflictions, and shalt not myself — one of their own kind — be moved? Though with their high wrongs I am struck to the quick, if they repent, my purpose doth extend not a frown further. Go, release them, Ariel. My charms I'll break, their sense I'll restore, and they shall be themselves."

"I'll fetch them, sir," said Ariel, and vanished.

With his staff Prospero traced a large circle on the ground. Where his staff passed it left a band of bright red on the green grass, that glowed even in the daylight. He stood at the center and considered his leather-bound book of spells. He had commanded elves of the hills and nymphs of the waters, demi-puppets, elemental spirits and those who make the midnight mushrumps. With their aid he had done deeds of power: dimmed the sun at noontime, set roaring war between the sea and sky, opened graves and called forth the dead. But these were not powers that belonged in the world of men. He must give them over if he would again be Duke of Milan.

"This rough magic I here reject, and once I have required this heavenly music —" he tapped his staff and solemn music played, that would unwind the charm about the King's men, "— why, I'll break my staff, bury it fathoms in the earth, and deeper than ever anchor did sound I'll drown my book."

Then came the King's party, as Ariel compelled. Into the clearing from the eastern way strode King Alonso, his face marked with pain, his hands tight clenched in the royal purple of his robe as if only thus could he keep from hammering at his own temples. Good Gonzalo went beside him in close attendance. Followed the wicked, sneering Sebastian and Antonio, in like manner attended by Adrian and Francisco. Walking as men who know not where they are nor where they go, they all entered the circle which Prospero had made, and there stood enchanted.

With his staff, Prospero traced a large circle on the ground.

The music played on, dissolving the charm slowly as the morning steals upon the night, melting the darkness. "A solemn air," said Prospero to the stiff, silent men who could not yet see or hear him. "The best comforter to cure thy brains, now useless, boiled within thy skull. There stand, for you are spell-stopped."

Prospero breathed deep as he beheld them. Here at last they were gathered: the good Gonzalo, his true preserver; the King Alonso, who sent the soldiers to capture Milan and overthrow Prospero; Sebastian, who led the soldiers, and Antonio, his very own brother, who had opened the gates to the invaders, and plotted with Sebastian to kill the King. Prospero read the repentance on Alonso's face, and sighed.

Prospero unfastened the clasp of his magic cloak. "Not one of them would know me. Ariel, fetch me the hat and rapier in my cell. I will present myself as I was sometime in Milan."

In a breath, Ariel had gone and come again, with Duke's robes for Prospero. Attiring him with all the splendor of the court, Ariel sang:

> *"Where the bee sucks, there suck I,*
> *In a cowslip's bell I lie.*
> *There I couch when owls do cry.*
> *On the bat's back I do fly*
> *After summer merrily.*
>
> *Merrily, merrily shall I live now*
> *Under the blossom that hangs on the bow."*

Prospero smiled to hear the song. "Why, that's my dainty Ariel," he said. "I shall miss thee, but yet thou shalt have freedom. So, so, so. To the King's ship, invisible as thou are. Thou shall find the mariners asleep under the hatches. The master and the boatswain being awake, bring them to this place, and presently, I pray."

Ariel cried, "I drink the air before me, and return before your pulse beat twice," and was away.

The solemn music played softer and softer. The glowing red circle faded into nothing. Slowly the members of the King's party began to move, slow and stiff as statues come new to life. Gonzalo croaked, a rusty sound, then said, "All torment, trouble, wonder, and amazement inhabits here. Some heavenly power guide us out of this fearful country!" Alonso stared about him.

Prospero's hour had come; he flung aside his cape and stood forward. "Behold, sir king," he said, "I am the wronged Duke of Milan, Prospero. For more proof that a living prince does now speak to thee, I embrace thy body." He clasped Alonso by the shoulders. "And to thee and thy company I bid a hearty welcome."

The King could scarce believe his eyes, the more so after being tormented by the Harpy. "Whether thou be he or no, I know not," he said. Then memory of his acts against Prospero rushed upon him, and clasping Prospero's arms in return, he exclaimed: "Thy dukedom I resign, and do entreat thou pardon me my wrongs."

Bowing to the King, Prospero turned to embrace old Gonzalo. He did the old man all respect due an honest soul in a world of slyboots. A look passed from Sebastian to Antonio, as they realized they still held their swords in hand, and that they had drawn them first to kill the King. Prospero saw that look, and spoke aside to them, so that the King would not hear. "But you, my brace of lords," he said, "were I so minded, I here could turn his Highness' frown upon you and condemn you traitors. At this time I will tell no tales."

All color drained from Sebastian's face. "The devil speaks in him," he whispered.

"No," replied Prospero, and held his eye until Sebastian slipped his blade into its scabbard. Antonio quickly sheathed his own weapon.

Prospero fronted the false Duke. "For you, most wicked sir, whom to call brother would infect my mouth, I do forgive thy rankest faults, all of them, and require my dukedom of thee, which I know thou must restore."

He held out his hand. Antonio, helpless, tugged the Duke's signet ring from off his finger, and handed it to Prospero.

"If thou be'st Prospero," said the King, "tell how thou hast met us here, wracked upon this shore, where I have lost — how sharp the pain of this remembrance is! — my dear son Ferdinand."

Prospero looked upon the King's mournful face and was moved. "I am woe to hear it, sir. Yet I myself have suffered the same loss."

"You the same loss?"

"As great to me, and as recent, and I have means much weaker than you may call to comfort you, for I have lost my daughter."

Alonso clapped hand to heart and groaned. "A daughter? O, heavens, that they were living both in Naples, the King and Queen there! I would give my life that it might be, I'd lie mudded in that oozy bed where my son lies. When did you lose your daughter?"

"In this last tempest." Alonso clasped him close in sorrow, and Prospero at last forgave him in his heart. Now would he lift the King's mourning. "Welcome, sir," he said. "This cell's my court. Here have I few attendants, and subjects none. Pray you, look in. Since my dukedom you have given me again, I will repay you with as good a thing, a wonder to content you as much as me."

Prospero threw wide the door to his cell. At first Alonso was astonished to see such a noble chamber on so wild an island. Then he beheld Ferdinand and Miranda, playing chess.

The King staggered back. "If this should prove a vision of the island," he said, his voice all hoarse with strong emotion, "one dear son shall I lose twice."

At the sound of his father's voice, Ferdinand sprang to his feet, and ran to kneel before him. "Though the seas threaten, they are merciful," he said. "I have cursed them without cause."

The King stretched out a trembling hand, and touched his son's face. Tears of joy filled his eyes. "Now, all the blessings of a glad father compass thee about! Arise, and say how thou came here."

Then stepped Miranda from the cell, dainty as a deer. When she saw the company of men assembled there, she was at first too shy to speak. But then she said, "O, wonder! How many goodly creatures are there here! O, brave new world that has such people in it!"

The King said to his son, "What is this maid with whom thou wast at play? Is she the goddess that hath cut us apart, then brought us thus together?"

"Sir, she is no goddess but mortal, and she's mine," proclaimed the Prince, drawing his lady-love to his side. "I chose her when I could not ask my father for his advice, nor thought I had one. She is the daughter of this famous Duke of Milan, of whom I have received a second life; and second father this lady makes him to me."

"I am hers," said Alonso. "But, O, how oddly will it sound that I must ask my child forgiveness!"

"There, sir, stop," broke in Prospero. "Let us not burden our remembrances with a heaviness that's gone."

"Give me your hands," said the King, and he blessed the young lovers.

Voices called, and through the eastern entry to the clearing came the Master of the King's ship, and with him the Boatswain. Ariel, unseen, had brought them.

Gonzalo laughed at sight of the Boatswain, and cried to the King, "O, look sir, look sir, here is more of us. I said this fellow was born to be hung and so could not drown. What is the news?"

Replied the Boatswain, "The best news is that we have safely found our King and company. The next: our ship, which we believed had split, is tight and bravely rigged as when we first put out to sea. We were but dead of sleep and — how we know not — all clapped under hatches."

"Sir, all this service have I done since I went," whispered Ariel.

"My tricksy spirit!" Prospero murmured back.

The King shook his head. "This is as strange a maze as ever men trod."

Prospero held up his hand. "Sir, do not infest your mind with beating on the strangeness of this business. At leisure, I'll explain these accidents; till then, be cheerful, and think of each thing well." He spoke aside to Ariel. "Come hither, spirit; set Caliban and his companions free. Untie the spell." Ariel flew off to do Prospero's bidding, knowing it must be near the last time. Meanwhile, Prospero said to King Alonso, "How fares my gracious sir? There are yet missing of your company some few odd lads that you remember not."

Then through the western entry ran the butler, the jester and the monster, sweating, jostling, squealing like pigs. Ariel drove them on, though none but Prospero could see. They collapsed in a heap in the center of the clearing, still wearing their stolen finery.

Monster Caliban crawled out of the pile and cowered at sight of Prospero. "O, these be brave spirits indeed! How fine my master is! I am afraid he will punish me."

Sebastian and Antonio made fun of the three. Prospero said, "Mark but the badges of these men, my lords, then say if they be true. These three have robbed me, and this demi-devil had plotted with them to take my life. Two of these fellows you must know and own." His eye fastened on Caliban. "This thing of darkness I admit is mine."

"I shall be pinched to death," moaned Caliban.

"Is this not Stephano, my drunken butler?" asked the King.

But Stephano had run so far and been pinched so often and so hard that every muscle in his body shrieked. "O, touch me not!" he pleaded. "I am not Stephano but a cramp."

Prospero looked him up and down. "You'd be king o' the isle, sirrah?" he demanded.

"I should have been a sore one, then," the butler groaned.

Alonso gaped at monster Caliban, with his bristling hair, his big crooked teeth and lumpy head. "This is as strange a thing as ever I looked on," he said.

"He is as awkward in his manners as in his shape," said Prospero. To Caliban he ordered, "Go, sirrah, to my cell. Take with you your companions. As you look to have my pardon, trim it handsomely."

Caliban looked at his master with more respect than was his custom. "Ay, that I will, and I'll be wise hereafter and seek for grace. What a thrice-double ass was I to take this drunkard for a god, and worship this dull fool!"

Alonso spoke to his servants. "Get you hence. Bestow those garments where you found them."

Prospero bowed to the King. "Sir, I invite your Highness and your train to my poor cell, where you shall take your rest for this one night. And in the morn I'll bring you to your ship, and so to Naples, where I have hope to see the marriage of these our dear beloved solemnized."

Alonso clasped his hand. "I long to hear the story of your life, which must take the ear strangely."

Prospero bowed again. "I promise you calm seas, and sail so quick that shall catch up your royal fleet far off." Aside to Ariel he whispered, "My Ariel, chick, that is thy charge. Then to the elements be free, my bird, and fare thou well." To the others he said, "Please you, draw near."

Ferdinand and Miranda passed first into the cell, the King himself giving way to them. He followed after, with Gonzalo and the other lords and gentlemen. At last Prospero stood alone in the clearing, without his staff, or magic cloak, or book of spells. He looked up into the evening sky where Ariel played joyous games with the birds returning to their nests. Then Prospero spoke these words, though whether to Ariel, or to the gods, or to some unseen playhouse audience none could tell. He said:

"Now my charms are overthrown,
And what strength I have's mine own,
Which is most faint. Now 'tis true
I must be here confined by you,
Or sent to Naples. Let me not,
Since I have my dukedom got
and pardoned the deceiver, dwell
in this bare island by your spell,
But release me from my bands
With the help of your good hands.
Gentle breath of yours my sails
Must fill, or else my project fails.
And my ending is despair,
Unless I be relieved by prayer.
As you from crimes would pardoned be,
Let your indulgence set me free."

~ *The End* ~

AFTERWORD

Prospero gave up his magic, but the theatre is alive with it. When Harpy Ariel makes the banquet vanish, but leaves the table behind, this is stage magic. Shakespeare, in his stage directions, says it shall be done, "with a quaint device," though no record remains of what the device was or how it operated. Such things had been part of the theatre for a long time, and would be built specially for the needs of a particular play. In 1536, for a French mystery play, a mechanic made a severed head that would jump three times across the stage.

In Shakespeare's day, every stage had to have a trap door or two. The Harpy might come up from a trap door, as if from the Underworld. And Juno might descend from the heavens, for every stage had a windlass in the overhead, with which angels and gods could descend to earth and rise again.

Frequently these entrances and exits were accompanied by thunder, or blasts on trumpets, because the windlass creaked and the rope groaned. Thunder and lightning were frequently used sound effects. They added punch to an entrance, or heralded an important statement or action. The sound of thunder was produced in various ways; some theatres rolled iron balls in a wooden trough up in the overhead, some rolled a barrel of stones, some rattled large sheets of copper.

With only lamps and candles for stage lighting, the lightning flash was harder to recreate. If the flash was important to the story, it might be done with a firecracker. Sounds, especially loud sounds were used for punctuation, and to direct attention. Cannons, firecrackers, trumpets, drums or whistles would focus the audience where needed for best effect.

Special effects were not without hazards in Shakespeare's day. On the 29th of June, 1613, at a performance of his last play, *Henry VIII*, a cannon was fired to salute the entry of the player King. Sparks from the cannon landed on the thatched roof of the theatre. The dry reeds flared up quickly. All the people had to scramble to safety through two narrow doors. No one was injured, but one man's pants did catch fire. He doused the flames with beer.

Music might also be used as a special effect. It is in *The Tempest*. When invisible musicians start to play, the music is an actor in the drama. But the best kind of effects are the ones the audience members create in their own minds. When Ariel is on-stage and yet supposed to be invisible; when the King's party stands spellbound in Prospero's magic circle, while he walks among them unseen: there is no effect here, but that kind which makes the theatre magic. The players have said, "Let's pretend," and the audience has said, "We will."

★ NOTE: The dialogue in quotes is based upon
    Edward Staunton's edition (November 1857-May 1860).
    It has been abridged and amended to fit the shorter narrative form.

GLOSSARY

AFFLICTION • pain, distress or suffering

BOATSWAIN • pronounced "bo-sun," the sailor in charge
of all sails and rigging on a ship

BRINE • salty water

BUTT • a large barrel or cask; 126 gallons

DOUBLET • a man's close-fitting jacket, with or without sleeves

DRUDGERY • work that is hard, lowly or tiresome

FATHOM • a unit of measure at sea; six feet

JERKIN • a short jacket or vest

MIDNIGHT
MUSHRUMPS • a country word for mushrooms that grow up overnight

MOONCALF • a born fool

NYMPHS • nature goddesses, beautiful maidens dwelling
in rivers, trees, mountains or the sea

ORACLE • a place or person which brings forth
the wisdom of the gods

PLAGUE • a terrible disease

POX • a disease which marks the skin, as in chicken pox

PRATTLE • to talk much or foolishly

PROPHECIES • declarations or predictions of the future

SACK • a strong Spanish wine

SIMPLETON • a person who is stupid or is easily deceived

TRENCHERING • trenchers - wooden boards on which to serve food

TYRANT • a cruel ruler

UNDAUNTED • not hesitating because of fear or discouragement

VEXATION • a cause of annoyance or trouble

WHIST • silence

PETER V.T. KAHLE's first book in this series, *Shakespeare's A Midsummer Night's Dream: A Prose Narrative,* was a finalist for the Small Press Book Award in 1997. Kahle has been a teacher, a stained glass artist, and a lacrosse referee. He is a past president of the Pacific Northwest Writers Association, a member of the Literary Arts Alliance and a founder of the Collective Wheee. He speaks at schools and libraries on topics including writing and Shakespeare. This is his second book for young people. He lives in Seattle, Washington, with his wife, Lani.

BARBARA NICKERSON's enchanting watercolor illustrations grew out of a long fascination with Shakespeare. She has shown her work in New York, Germany, and had a solo exhibition in Paris. She is listed in both the *Encyclopedia of Sumi-E* and *Who's Who in International Sumi-E Artists.* She received her BFA at the Art Institute of Chicago, and is a workshop teacher and signature member of the Northwest Watercolor Society, Women Painters of Washington and Puget Sound Sumi Artists. This is her second book for Seventy Fourth Street Productions. Barbara lives on a ranch in Cle Elum, Washington, with her husband, Jul.

THE TEMPEST was set in a variation of Bembo,
a text type noted for its classical beauty and readability.
Bembo was modeled on type cut by Francesco Griffo in
Venice, Italy, in 1495. It takes its name from its first use in
Aldus Manutius' printing of *De Aetna* by Pietro Bembo.
A standard typeface in Europe since its origin, Bembo
was redesigned for the Monotype Corporation in 1929
and digitized in 1990 for Adobe Systems, Inc.

Design and production by
Deb Figen, ART & DESIGN SERVICE
Seattle, Washington

Printed in Korea by Amica International
on acid-free paper